HEAVY TRUCK

CHRIS PARK

HEAVY TRUCK

OSPREY

Published in 1982 by Osprey Publishing Limited,
12–14 Long Acre, London WC2E 9LP
Member company of the George Philip Group

British Library Cataloguing in Publication Data

Park, Chris
    Heavy truck.
    1. Commercial vehicles—History
    I. Title
    629.2'24   TL230
ISBN 0-85045-464-6

Editor Tim Parker
Designed by Roger Daniels

Filmset and printed by BAS Printers Limited,
Over Wallop, Hampshire

Contents

1 Rail and canal onslaught

Dawn over Shap . . . rival routes . . . glamorous White . . . steam on the road . . . railways a mistake? . . . tractors first . . . trucks later . . . external versus internal combustion . . . the army decides . . . and offers money . . . switch to petrol . . . orthodoxy arrives . . . and stays . . . taxation, registration and licensing . . . no favours given.

Modern trucking in the UK. The American Mack cabover is registered in France but is hauling a trailer for a British based company and is shot here, travel stained, in a motorway service area

First light came almost imperceptibly, greying the eastern sky as we ran swiftly towards the border at Gretna Green. As our truck, all thirty two tons of her, hammered on down the final miles of the A74 the greyness turned to gold and the splendour of the new dawn in Scotland gave every promise of a fine day to come in England. Riding a full eight feet above road level I could see mist low-lying on the Solway Firth and caught glimpses of dancing silver as it thinned to reveal the shining surface of the sea. Then we rumbled on to the broader carriageway of the M6, swinging away to the east as it skirted the still-sleeping town of Carlisle. A roadside sign warned of 'slow lorries', but we climbed contemptuously to the top

of the long grade with no noticeable drop in speed, the growl of the Rolls-Royce diesel deepening as Bob progressively poured in the power.

Soon the long curves of the motorway switched to the opposite tack, twitching its direction slightly westwards to take us far enough from the smaller town of Penrith to leave its drowsy citizens in peace. We swept on south in company with the old A6 trunk road and the main line railway. The tarmac trunk route mostly followed the natural lie of the land, climbing steeply and spasmodically as motorway and railway carved their expensively engineered courses steadily and easily upwards. Over to the west the Lakeland hills were still shrouded in mist, and with no distant views to admire I found myself concentrating on scanning the two rival routes whenever they came into sight. I saw only one vehicle travelling the A6, a big tipper probably hauling out of the local quarries, and only one train, a short line of grubby wagons attached to a dirty, smoking diesel loco. Not for the first time was I struck by the emptiness of the old ways through the mountains, to all intents and purposes devoid of traffic while M6, even at that early hour, teemed with life, taking on the appearance of a great conveyor belt carrying people, metal and merchandise across the ancient hills with scarcely a pause in the purposeful flow.

'Just look at that! Ain't she beautiful.' Bob's voice, pitched only a little above normal conversational level, came clearly across the expanse of comfortable cab between us. He went on: 'I reckon he must polish those chromed stacks at every truck stop.'

The 'stacks' in question were the glistening, sky-wards pointing exhaust pipes rearing behind the cab of a White Road Commander cresting the climb to Shap summit from the south. By now the sun had cleared away the lingering mist and the oncoming truck was bathed in golden light as it slipped swiftly by, and we saw that from the cab top spoiler to the very tail end of the slab-sided reefer the whole rig was immaculate.

'But it's hardly our style, is it?', I commented, perhaps a little enviously.

'No, but things are definitely going that way,' Bob said. 'I certainly wouldn't swop this cab for his, though I'd love to have a couple of those stacks, dozens of marker lights and a really ritzy paint job. We've got good, efficient motors now, so what we need is a bit of style in trucking. I mean something beyond the customary pair of air horns and battery of fog lamps. People should be made to be as fascinated by the big trucks as they seem to be by the old railway engines. They should also be taught that they owe them very much more'.

As he fell silent again I realized that his thoughts had been running parallel to mine. All those sobering glimpses of the lonely, rather pathetic looking railway tracks had set us wondering what might have been if the application of power to land transport had stayed where it began . . . on the roads. With steam having become so synonymous with railways, most people have forgotten that putting steam power on to rails was a second choice. It was also one that sent transport development down a very long, exceedingly blind alley. The resulting dinosaur is still with us, slimmed

Crossing the River Medway at Rochester in Kent two artics pass. One has come from France through Dover, the other is probably on its way out

down somewhat but possessing a mammoth appetite for resources which could be better used elsewhere.

A Frenchman named Cugnot is widely credited with the construction of the first known powered vehicle and pretty concrete evidence of this is available in the form of the original vehicle which somehow has survived. If it had been more successful it would probably have met with an untimely end like so many others that were actually made to run on the appalling tracks that passed for roads in every century but the present one. The Cugnot machine was a front wheel drive tricycle intended to earn its keep as an artillery tractor and can thus in a sense be classed as a

A typical motorway scene (M4). The crowded road is not unique to the UK, in fact, this could be anywhere in Europe. 'Ancient' Atkinson in the foreground, leads its modern brother, called Seddon Atkinson

goods vehicle. That was in 1769 and Cugnot was soon served with the 18th century equivalent of a prohibition order and his device locked away in a Paris arsenal, which is another reason for its surprising survival.

Once invented, the horseless carriage, or, as it happened, the horseless tractor, could not be uninvented, as the horse owners were to discover. But they tried very hard for almost a century in England to keep steam machines off the so-called roads. After Cugnot there was something of a lull but then the production and operation of steam carriages went on apace and, despite the unsuitability of running surfaces that were no more than rutted tracks, powered passenger carrying vehicles enjoyed considerable commercial success before the first steam hauled passenger trains ran. The railways, of course, were destined to win the 19th century transport battle with consummate ease purely because the horse owners managed to get the hated new vehicles legislated out of existence. In the prevailing circumstances, it was probably not surprising that no-one appeared to realise that the laying down of the wonderful new iron roads was even then an outrageous irrelevance. At any rate, there seemed to be few voices pointing out that the railway's inability to provide door to door transport was an impossible obstacle to achieving viability except in a few favoured situations. So there followed the onset of speculation that rapidly grew to manic proportions. While the already appalling roads were allowed to decay to virtual extinction, railway mania became a widespread affliction that persuaded a normally sober, careful citizenry to pour truly incalculable amounts of wealth into a whole host of railway projects. It is no exaggeration to say that only those with a very considerably elastic imagination could persuade themselves that the new lines would ever serve any sort of useful purpose, let alone earn a commercial return on the money spent.

The story of overland transport would have been very different if the men of vision had thought along more rational lines and persuaded the men of money to finance the building of roads capable of carrying powered vehicles with reasonable reliability and speed. But George Stephenson was said to be a simple man and it seems likely that the apparent simplicity and undeniable durability of the iron road led him and his ilk to overlook the real achilles heel of the new system. This was the sheer inability of the steel tyred wheels to grip the smooth rails tenaciously enough to enable a load to be hauled up anything other than the gentlest of gradients. Hence the essential construction of numerous tunnels, high embankments, deep cuttings and dizzy viaducts wherever the terrain was anything other than reasonably level. There is no doubt that the cost in terms of both lives and money would have been more than enough to finance the construction of a real road system, one that could never have become the mill-stone the railways turned out to be. Moreover, there would have been no need for the road builders to go to extreme lengths to smooth out gradients, and construction to quite modest and relatively inexpensive standards would have been sufficient to improve communications to an extent which the comparatively sparse and unplanned rail system could never have begun to match. So the costly and wildly inefficient railway era need never have been. There

must be additional irony in the fact that the nation which invented railways and willed the construction of so many miles of unprofitable track probably needed them least, if at all. And my ride over Shap Fells on a purpose-built road that sparked off this speculation could have been a commonplace trip as long as a hundred years ago. History suggests that road vehicle development would certainly have kept pace with the provision of better and better running surfaces, just as it has throughout the present century.

But the Victorians were understandably dazzled by the high speeds attainable on rails though they must have remained highly conscious of their continuing dependence on the horse and the roads that took them to their own front doors. In Victorian times there were three and a half million horses alive in England, most of them involved in road transport of one sort or another. The railways were totally dependent on them for bringing passengers and goods to the stations, very many of which were quite remote from the populations and industries they were meant to serve. It was, however, the horse owners who actively impeded the development of powered road transport by contriving to bring in restrictive legislation designed to keep the speeds of horseless road vehicles down to no more than a walking pace. Thus the horse as prime mover on the roads was reprieved for half a century during which time the mad proliferation of railways ensured that many of the lines built were utterly uneconomic and ready to die at the very first hint of external competition.

The railways did, however, succeed in killing off the heavy truck of the day. Since the middle ages this had been the inter-city multi-horse wagon. Somehow their operators managed to keep the loads moving over

ABOVE: *Dated as 1769 this Cugnot 'Fardier' was a practical method of 'heavy' haulage. The driver sat on the box in the centre and steered with the two-handed tiller*

ABOVE RIGHT: *In 1897 Daimler in Germany produced this very modern looking truck. They could have promoted rear wheel brakes, shaft drive and considerable driver control*

RIGHT: *A year earlier in 1896 Daimler's lorry looked a lot like this. Although of lighter weight, the company had learnt a lot in that single year*

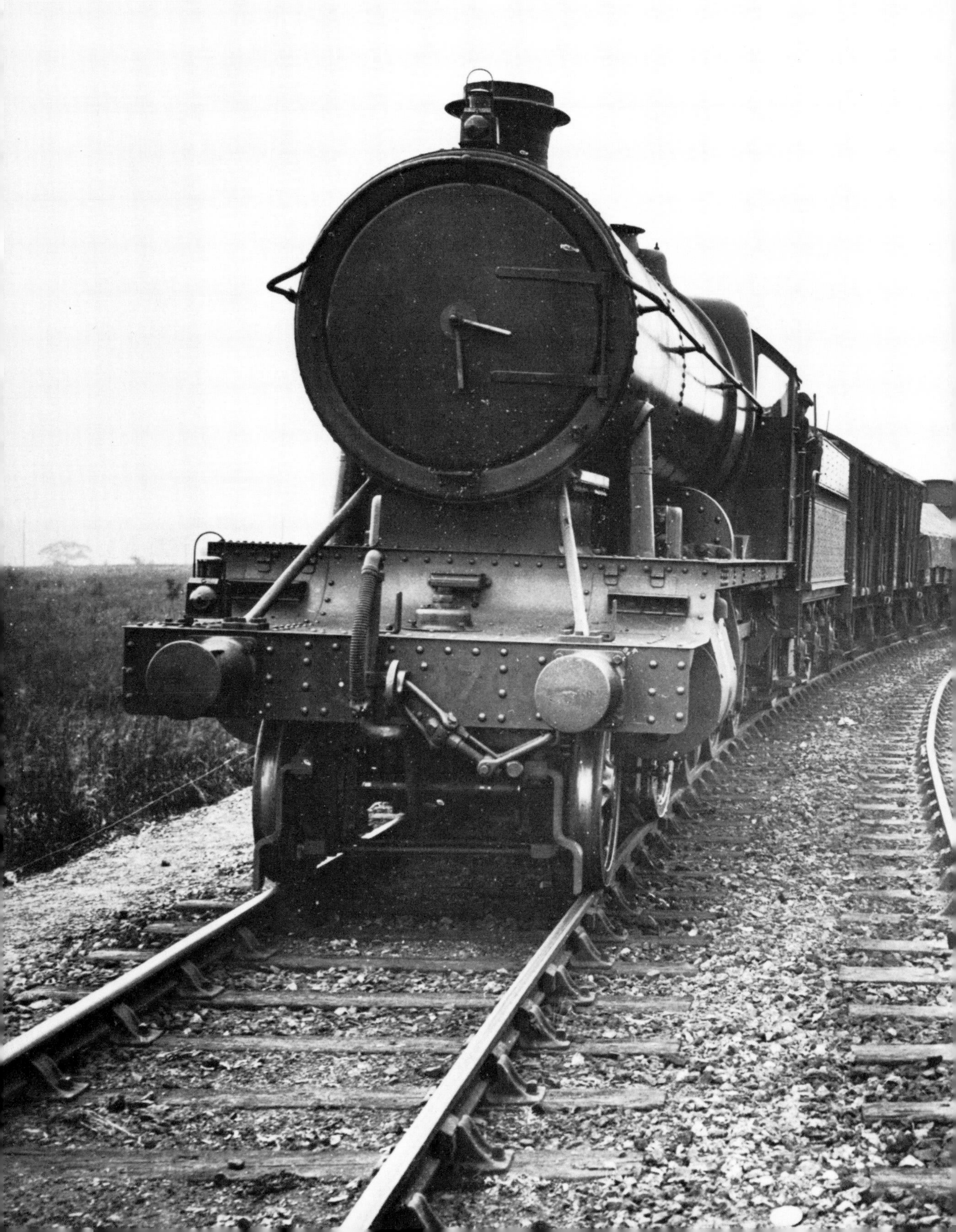

The Age of the Train? Even in 1912 when this shot of a mixed goods train leaving Greenford in West London was taken, the railways were already losing out to the crudest, most legislated against road vehicle of all, the steam tractor. At the turn of the century, both horse-drawn and steam-powered barges still carried lucrative, specialized cargoes like coal and grain, but the canal network was dying, doomed to extinction by that same, crippling inflexibility which the railway speculators overlooked. The steam barge pictured below could bring you 200 tons of coal at one go, but only if you lived on the banks of a canal

1901 and steam power was very common. This Thornycroft was typical with its 'shaft' drive and solid wheels

Foden was another well-known manufacturer of steam wagons. This 1909 version uses chain drive and something more substantial as a driver's cab. Both trucks were used for local deliveries only

the always dreadful roads, eventually to be very much aided by the establishment of what can now be considered to be the equivalent of modern motorway service areas. These were staging points equipped with granaries, stables and warehouses. Then in the 18th century the growing canal network brought the first hot breath of competition and over many of the routes heavy loads began to be floated to their destinations, though the wagon was still a vital link in the transport chain just as it was to be during the railway era which was about to dawn. The canals, of course, shared the inflexibility of the railways, but together they managed to virtually eliminate all long hauls of heavy goods by road and heavy haulage operations then began to be mainly local ones centred on the canal basins and railheads. Even so, long road hauls had still to be undertaken in those regions untouched by the canal and railway networks.

By now the steam revolution had reached the farms in the guise of stationary engines which were used for ploughing and threshing. As these had to be moved about the farm it was logical to fit them with wheels, and it was then but a small step to make them self-propelled. Thus the steam tractor was born, or, more accurately, re-born. Nearly a century before, Cugnot had constructed his steam tractor, so credit where credit is due. The new tractors, however, were actually able to haul things and the traction engine, as it was known, was soon further developed for road usage to produce a variant more accurately described as a road locomotive. This was put to the job of hauling the really heavy loads over Britain's still wholly inadequate road system.

Despite being hampered by the spiteful provisions of the 1865 Locomotive Act which set speed limits of two mph in towns, a dizzy four mph in the country, the road locomotive with its ability to haul loads as great as 60 tons began to offer very serious competition to its counterpart on rails. The speed limits, in fact, were quite superfluous as the notorious man with the red flag was required to walk in front. Although the red flag was dispensed with in 1876, the pedestrian retarder remained mandatory until what is now known as the Emancipation Act was passed in 1896. Then the Heavy Motor Car Act of 1903 legalised the one-man operation of road locomotives weighing less than five tons unladen and raised the relevant speed limit to five mph. This measure significantly changed the direction of development, favouring a lighter vehicle than the locomotive and one capable of carrying rather than hauling. Thus the steam wagon, a truck rather than a tractor, began its domination of the road haulage scene. With it came many names that were to become famous in their day, Atkinson, Foden and Leyland are three that have survived into the modern world of trucks.

So steam on rails began to suffer very considerably from the mounting competition of steam on the roads. But the latter was soon fighting for its very existence. The fight was to be to the death, external combustion being challenged by internal combustion. As early as 1896, motor car pioneer Gottlieb Daimler had begun to produce petrol-driven trucks, many of which were imported into Britain. The 20th century dawned and soon the run-up to World War I began. The army had for a long time

LEFT AND BELOW: *Petrol driven Daimler of 1912. The shape of things to come is set. The driver still needs a proper cab. The truck below onto which a Bristol Fighter is being mounted uses both shaft and chain drive. Contemporary car design is still an influence with the screen and lamps*

used steam tractors for hauling heavy guns and with war obviously in the offing military men began to consider the possibility of widening their use of powered transport. A full scale assessment of the relative merits of steam and petrol propelled trucks was undertaken. Extensive field trials produced results that made internal combustion a clear winner.

From then on the War Office began to offer subsidies to petrol-powered truck operators who undertook to supply a vehicle, complete with driver, for military use at 48 hours notice. This was a body blow for the steam wagon constructors and a number of them made the logical move of switching to petrol powerplants. The correctness of the army's choice was proved beyond doubt during the long years of war, but it should be said that on the home front steam wagons put up a great performance. It was, in fact, the type's finest hour and the future could promise no more than a slow but steady decline.

Although the truck story begins with Cugnot and his rather original ideas on chassis layout, automotive orthodoxy eventually began to be represented by vehicles which were to remain virtually unchanged in basic design right up to the present day. Clearly, anything that Cugnot devised had to be original, yet originality was not a strong point of many of the subsequent designs because they were based on existing horse drawn vehicles. This can even be said of the traction engine which was developed from the horse-drawn stationary steam engine. Strict modernity came in with the steam wagon with its normally front mounted powerplant driving the rear wheels, a layout soon adopted almost universally by its petrol driven rivals. The only prominent mechanical feature of many of the earliest trucks that was to disappear within a relatively few years was the driving chain. With this gone in favour of the open propellor shaft, there was little disagreement on the components preferred and on how to dispose them about the ladder-type chassis frame, and since then no-one seems to have felt strongly compelled to try swopping things around. So the front mounted engine still sits above the live front axle located by leaf springs shackled to the chassis above. A dry plate clutch connects engine and gearbox and an open propellor shaft takes the drive to a differential unit housed in a live rear axle also located by leaf springs. A masterpiece of modern technology? Hardly! A machine so archaic in design that it simply can't be true? Not really. An amazing amalgam of the two that happens to do its job more efficiently than anything else yet thought of? Well, perhaps. But it is really up to the reader to decide for himself if and when he gets to the end of the book.

Meanwhile, it is necessary to keep constantly in mind the political and economic climates in which this apparently stunted development has taken place. Some years before the war to end war had actually begun, the government had started to take serious notice of the escalating expansion of the road vehicle population. The Development and Road Improvement Funds Act had been designed by Lloyd George to make vehicle users provide the finance needed to build new roads and improve existing ones. So at last it was officially recognised that the nation really needed roads. The Road Fund was set up in 1909, the money being collected by

19

imposing both licensing and petrol duties, the latter being levied at half rate for commercial vehicles. Then in 1920 a new system of taxation, registration and licensing was introduced under the Roads Act of that year. From the first day of 1921, goods vehicles were taxed on unladen weight and the tax on fuel was abolished. Everyone knows that this was

A Daimler road train in India in 1910. The first 'trailer' is a carriage (even labelled as 'third class') followed by trucks, all of which are heavily influenced by

railway engineering. Even the style of the 'engine' adheres to the image. Interesting is the combination of people and goods haulage

one tax which refused to die. Once revived (by Winston Churchill in 1928), it had a more and more irresistible attraction for the greedy hands of government and road transport operators had to learn to expect no favours in this or, indeed, in any other matter concerning the carriage of goods by road.

World War 1 influenced road haulage very strongly. The truck's versatility under battle conditions persuaded many that its day was ready. These are Leyland WD trucks with solid rubber tyres and twin rear wheels

2 Road fights back, and wins

Peacetime battles continue . . . steam a long time dying . . . A, B, and C Licences . . . driving tests begin . . . tyres, taxation and technology . . . triumph of the oilers . . . life above the engine . . . cab-overs conventional . . . but bonnets preferred . . . the big names . . . nocturnal beasts . . . the great trunk routes . . . autobahn and autostrada . . . rumours of roads to come.

After the war the two commercial battles continued with ever increasing intensity—road versus rail with the former steadily but relentlessly taking a bigger and bigger share of the traffic—steam versus petrol with steam fighting a brave yet utterly hopeless rearguard action. Steam's total and final defeat was a long time coming, especially in the heavyweight class. Even as far on as 1926, 70 per cent of all trucks of more than five tons unladen weight were steam propelled and the actual manufacture of steam wagons did not finally cease in Britain until around the year 1950. Although over the years many relatively sophisticated steamers were produced, some of which could cruise at speeds as high as 50 mph and do this with incredible smoothness, the weight penalty imposed by having to carry water as well as fuel reduced payloads sufficiently to make viable operation difficult. In addition, steam raising before the day's work could begin took as long as an hour, and once on the road much more valuable time was lost in taking on water at intervals of no more than 30 or 40 miles. In very cold weather the prospect of the water freezing in the boiler, or more likely, in the supply tanks, was a constant worry.

Between the two world wars, legislation, as always, played a large part in determining the shape of the road transport industry. Truck designers had nearly always worked under the constraint of laws specifying overall dimensions, unladen and laden weights, individual axle loadings and so on, some or all of these being tied in with taxation levels and maximum permitted speeds. Then the 1933 Road Traffic Act introduced tight governmental control of the actual operation of road haulage. A system of licensing was instituted to regulate which operators could do what and where. Thus a haulier plying for hire had to apply for an 'A' Licence which, if granted, allowed him to find business anywhere he could. 'B' Licence holders were permitted to carry their own goods as well as plying for hire, but could operate only in particular areas. A 'C' Licence was granted as a right to an applicant intending to carry only his own goods. The 1933 Act also attempted to regulate driving hours and drivers' wages and saddled some operators with the task of keeping detailed records of their work patterns. A B Licence lasted for one year, an A Licence for two, and a C Licence for three, and when they came up for renewal competitors could oppose them by showing that adequate services

already existed in the area. The main opposition to the granting and renewal of Licences came from the railways. Initially this had the result of slightly reducing road transport's share of the total amount of goods carried, though in the long term the steady transfer of freight from rail to road carried on without any very noticeable hiccup.

1919, a 'modern' Thornycroft and a speed limit of 12 mph. Mr Arding, or is it Mr Hobbs, ready for work. These trucks were large in stature. Little fundamental is going to change from now on

The aim of the licensing legislation was, in fact, to ease the competitive pressure on the railways. This was the motive that seven years previously had inspired Winston Churchill to raid the Road Fund. Then he had openly declared that he did not wish to see motor transport grow too quickly at the expense of the railways. After the first world war, government interference in the setting of the freight rates charged by the railways had rapidly proved disastrous. The newly-formed Ministry of Transport decreed at first that the charges should be upped sufficiently to make the railways able to pay their way. Then the Railway Rates Tribunal was set the task of fixing charges designed to raise a predetermined or target revenue. The Tribunal took almost ten years to do its sums, and then apparently failed to take into account the steady growth of competition from road transport. The result was that not one of the railway companies, by then amalgamated into four big groups, ever managed to hit its revenue target.

Meanwhile a Royal Commission had been set up, presumably to try to carve some sort of path of sanity through the growing transport jungle. Its main recommendation was the licensing of road haulage, as

RIGHT: *An early cabover Leyland, just post war. Side curtains would complete a true cab. The solid rubber used as tyres is getting thicker*

subsequently brought about by the 1933 Act. The final report included some rather pious comments on the desirability of co-ordinating all forms of transport, but little was said on how this should be done. The three left-wing members of the Commission did, however, rather predictably suggest that the transport industry should be put under some sort of public control.

The 1934 Road Traffic Act was more concerned with safety than with dealing further damaging blows at road transport operators. This was the important measure that made driving tests compulsory for all new drivers. Those who wished to drive Heavy Goods Vehicles were required to take a special test for which there was a minimum age limit of twenty one. HGVs were defined as rigid trucks weighing more than three tons unladen, and all articulated vehicles regardless of their unladen weights. This Act also brought in the built-up area speed limit of 30 mph that has persisted unchanged to the present day. In those days this limit was only of academic interest to the HGV driver as he was limited to 20 mph on all roads, a restriction that was to endure unchanged for the next 23 years. Even when it was finally changed, the HGV driver staying just legal through a built-up area was unable to accelerate at the derestriction sign without immediately breaking the law.

During the period when all this was taking place, legislation was also being used, somewhat paradoxically in the light of previous policies, to encourage the adoption of technological improvements in vehicle design.

This 1927 Leyland Hippo shows longer rigid construction, twin rear axles and the same cab style as the earlier cabover. Still 12 mph

Interesting contemporary scene, circa 1924, with a Karrier tanker pump-testing at Wandsworth in South London. Still no driver comfort of any consequence

Thus, high taxes and low speed limits were imposed to speed the demise of the solid rubber tyre. As late as 1910 the standard truck tyre was the thin steel band shrunk on to a wooden rim, a strict carry-over from horse-drawn vehicle practice. Rubber tyres were an optional extra and despite the availability of pneumatic tyres from about 1912, solids, as they came to be known, were, in various guises, the normal wear on trucks for upwards of 20 years. The authorities preferred pneumatics because they were so much kinder to road surfaces. Apart from giving both roads and vehicle loads and chassis a hard time, solids were prone to overheating to the extent that they could develop a molten core and consequently collapse. Nevertheless, tyre life could be as much as a far from insignificant 60,000 miles. For a long time it was common practice to employ pneumatics only on the front wheels. By the beginning of the thirties, however, pneumatics had virtually won the day and from 1933 solids were outlawed on new vehicles.

Another bout of differential taxation which actually discriminated against the fitting of diesel engines in trucks was, rather inexplicably, introduced in 1934. Not surprisingly this soon bit the dust, being repealed only a year later. At the same time the rate of Licence duty on the heaviest vehicles was increased savagely, a measure that set truck manufacturers on an intensive search for ways of reducing unladen weights, a quest they are still carrying on today with undiminished vigour.

The diesel engine (in Britain then known as the oil engine) itself imposed a considerable weight penalty on the trucks in which it was installed. This did not prevent diesels from rapidly taking over from petrol engines once the 'oiler' had shown what it could do. The first diesel engines in everyday use were massive stationary units exhibiting characteristics that apparently made them far from ideal for automotive applications. A great deal of development had to take place before lighter, higher revving diesels began to prove that the type could be used successfully as a vehicle powerplant. More correctly known as compression ignition engines, diesel units cost more to build than spark-ignited types burning petrol but have a much longer life and a more trouble-free one. The absence of an electrical ignition system enables the ci engine to avoid many of the road-side breakdowns suffered by petrol burners, especially when conditions are very wet.

Of more importance then, as now, was the efficiency of the diesel in converting fuel into power, and when operators in the thirties began to be confronted with improvements in fuel economy of the order of 60 to 70 per cent it was not surprising that their conversion to the new 'oilers' was pretty swift. Very many of them found it worthwhile to re-engine existing trucks, and when new ones had to be bought they invariably patronised those makers who were offering the diesel as an option. Soon it became the standard rather than the option, some manufacturers making their own, others offering to fit the products of one or more of the specialist engine builders. Among the latter it was, perhaps, the Manchester firm of L. Gardner & Sons that made the greatest contribution to the change-over, rapidly acquiring for its automotive diesels a reputation for

reliability and long life which soon persuaded operators and drivers that at long last they were on to a good thing. The other British diesel success story, that of Perkins, began in 1932 when derv was 5*d* per gallon and petrol 1*s* 4*d*.

By 1939, when the development of civilian road transport was for the second time brought to a halt by war, there were about half a million goods vehicles in use in Britain. Of these, about 10,000 were diesel-powered, and this figure can be taken as a fairly reliable indication of the number of heavy trucks then on the road. It seems that by then all

ABOVE: *An early artic. The date's 1927 but the AEC is an even earlier model converted from rigid 3 tons to perhaps an articulated 5 tons*

LEFT: *1928 Karrier of all of 10 tons! Truck is shod with early Dunlop SS Cord pneumatics. Coach painting and sign writing is superb*

RIGHT, AND ABOVE RIGHT: *As a final reminder, these two shots show metal rims (right) versus solid rubber, chain drive versus shaft and no sophistication versus the beginnings. The date is 1902 for the Thornycroft on the right and 1908 for the Dennis at the top*

Rigid plus draw bar trailer in 1930. This AEC cabover sets the pace for the next 50 years! Full electric lighting and side windows, at last

possible permutations and combinations of vehicle design had been tried and tested and there was nothing of a revolutionary nature remotely in the offing. Anyone who had ever operated, driven or ridden in the typical heavy truck of the day knew that there had to be refinements to come, but could see little obvious scope for significantly changing chassis layouts, suspension or transmission systems, while in the engine room King Diesel was clearly set for a very long reign. There was no such apparent certainty about how the operation of road transport would be influenced by outside political and commercial interests when once the war was over.

Naturally a great deal of truck refining had gone on between the wars, some of it concerned with the creature comforts of the driver and his mate. The days of the crew sitting unprotected in an open cab were gone. Comfort was hardly an apt word to describe what the thirties' cab could provide, but at least it had become relatively weatherproof. Apart from the fairly primitive seating which did little to cushion the normally bone-shattering ride, noise was perhaps the greatest bugbear. Until the advent of the diesel, some trucks had boasted engines of surprising mechanical quietness, one or two could be described as being almost silky in operation because of the way the power poured in with little attendant

1933 AEC pantechnicon and draw bar trailer. Contrast with the other methods . . .

roughness, but the same could not be said of the average transmission. Gearboxes could produce growls, wails and whines which were not easy for many ears to tolerate, final drives could be almost as bad, and when the diesel arrived the familiar knock and vibration came with it. In some ways this alleviated the situation by drowning all but the shrillest whines. Though the overall noise level increased it was more easily tolerated. However, the rest of the vehicle generated plenty more decibels to add to the cacophony, the very pliable chassis and bodywork emitting a variety of sounds ranging from the irritating chatter of ill-fitting windows and doors to quite ferocious crashings and banging keeping time with the very restricted movements of the stiffly suspended running gear.

Forward control was the order of the day for most of the heavies, restrictions on overall vehicle length had put load space at a premium so the driver was pushed as far forward as possible. Living on top of the engine was uncomfortably hot in summer and uncomfortably cold on the chillier winter days, the only heater being the engine itself, the warm air being ducted through the cracks around its poorly secured cover. With it came very undesirable fumes. The cab-over style obviously gave the man at the wheel a good view of the road but at the same time brought him much nearer to a frontal impact, not a particularly nice prospect in a cab

31

that was generally of quite flimsy construction. It also seriously reduced engine accessibility and it would have been no consolation to the mechanics of the day to have known that somebody, somewhere, was almost certainly experimenting with tilting the cab forward in the manner so widely used today. Certainly the first sleeper cab had already appeared in Europe in the shape of an Italian innovation on a six ton Fiat.

For some unfathomable reason, bonneted trucks are still regarded as normal or conventional designs, but particularly on this side of the Atlantic this is far from being true, nor has it been so for very many years. In Europe forward control is the norm. Cabovers are conventional. Yet according to the result of a survey carried out in 1973 by Magirus Deutz (now the German half of Iveco) and published in the Swiss magazine *Camion*, 57 per cent of the 2000 customers asked to state their preference for either normal or forward control plumped for the bonneted style. They gave their reasons as (1) better protection in collisions (2) more interior space (3) the convenience of bigger doors (4) ease of getting in and out. The fact remains that Magirus Deutz, along with all the other European makers, sell more forward control than normal control models, so it seems that commercial considerations rank higher than driver safety and convenience. There is something to be said, however, for the counter

LEFT: . . . *Guy 6 ton 'forward control' (with body by Caffyn's). Long rigid box van, difficult to manoeuvre. The Austin 7 with standard van body was the 1930s' Mini van. Contrast with . . .*

argument asserting that there are more cost-effective ways of giving the driver added protection than by sacrificing a considerable amount of valuable load space. Some authorities would argue that giving the driver the best possible view of the road is the most effective protection. Others say that making the driver vulnerable is the one sure way of making him careful.

Oddly enough, the earliest cabovers were mostly steam wagons and for a considerable period after the first world war steamers generally carried the heaviest payloads. These ranged from five to 10 tons. During the late twenties and throughout the thirties load capacities steadily increased until the mainly diesel engined heavies were capable of carrying loads of 15 to 20 tons by the time Germany decided to take on the rest of the world

BELOW: . . . the box van of the 1980s. This Daf refrigerated trailer can haul six times the weight. Fifty years' development seems to be missing

for the second time. Permissible axle loadings were always a limiting factor, one that naturally led to axle proliferation. The articulated type of vehicle was already well established, thanks mainly to the pioneering work of Scammell. The Watford firm always exhibited a great deal of ingenuity in making the best possible use of the legal requirements concerning weights and dimensions and adopted the artic layout to keep down axle loadings. But the Scammell artics were, in fact, flexible single vehicles with three axles, and a fourth could be added without difficulty. They were important environmentally in that they looked and behaved like artics. It is not hard to imagine the size and bitterness of the furore that would result today if the artic had just emerged as a new type of truck. Rigid trucks of those days generally had two or three axles, then came the advent of the second steering axle to make the four axle rigid a reality. For fairly obvious reasons this is sometimes known as the 'eight legger' or 'rigid eight'.

Apart from Scammell, the big names in big truck manufacture were Leyland and AEC. Unlike the situation in the passenger car industry, there was no sharp polarisation of truck making into one particular region. Leyland hailed from Lancashire, AEC and Scammell were based in the Home Counties, AEC to the west of London at Southall, Scammell to the north in Watford. There was one Scottish manufacturer, Albion. Guy, in Wolverhampton, was housed fairly close to the centre of the car industry while Sentinel, the steam wagon specialists, built their trucks 30 miles away to the west in the more rural surroundings of Shrewsbury. sentinel Works is now one of the addresses of Rolls-Royce who make truck diesel engines where steam once ruled. Maudslay, Thornycroft and Karrier were also well enough known names, but were slowly sliding into obscurity. Then, the names that dominate today's top weight truck scene, Scania, Volvo, Daf, Mercedes and so on, meant nothing to either the

ABOVE: *Heavy truck. 1935 Scammell and low loader shows off some interesting engineering philosophy. Tractor has chain drive to solid rubber tyred axle. Trailer has solid rubber too. Why?*

ABOVE RIGHT: *In stark contrast, the Scammell six wheeled tanker of 1935 is wearing giant pneumatics. Should be kinder to the tank*

RIGHT: *Circa 1939 scene. Two Thornycroft Sturdys illustrate AA membership(!) and extra front 'sign boards'. The cab style was already set for a good 30 years*

LEFT: *The inter-war years enabled Mercedes-Benz to develop this common style of truck. In 1939 the L2000 proudly showed off diesel power.*

RIGHT: *Conventional or normal control persisted longer in Europe. This 1937 Tatra T85 tanker shows Czechoslovakia's influence*

BELOW: *By contrast, some 40 years later, Europe and Britain are much closer. This Volvo was assembled in Britain – a suitable marriage of Swedish and British technology*

by-standers, the drivers or the operators. In fact, the first Daf truck had not yet been made.

The long haul trucks of the inter-war years were truly nocturnal beasts which, in the main, spent their working lives rolling along the great trunk routes. During the winter months their journeys would begin and end under cover of darkness. In summer the exodus from the big towns and cities began during the final hour or so of daylight. Only then could you get a clear sight of the Leylands, Scammells, AECs, Fodens and other makes beginning their long night hauls. The intermittent procession would be made up of six wheelers, eight wheelers, occasional artics, and rigids towing four wheeled trailers (drawbar outfits). Out in the night-blanketed countryside identification of the dark shapes behind the probing headlamp beams was difficult. Illuminated panels above some of the cabs advertised the names of the best-known operators and often gave away the identity of the truck behind the lights. In the absence of noise from lesser traffic, not as rare a circumstance as it is now, an educated ear could often detect marque-identifying sounds like the muted swish of Scammell driving chains, the painfully high-pitched whine of Karrier straight cut gears, the characteristic exhaust throb of the few petrol burners still employed on trunking.

The first Trunk Roads Act, passed in 1936, transferred to the care of the Ministry of Transport 4505 miles of main roads. This actually meant that the Ministry took complete financial responsibility for the chosen highways. It was only ten years since some sort of order had been put into road classification by the adoption of a numbering system that has survived more or less intact to the present day. As every road user knows, or should know, Class 1 roads were given numbers prefixed by the letter 'A', Class 2 roads numbers with a 'B' prefix, while the remainder, accounting for the major part of all road mileage, remained unclassified. The main through routes radiating from London were given the low A numbers—A1 went to the most celebrated route of all, the Great North Road which linked London and Edinburgh, A2 was given to the Dover

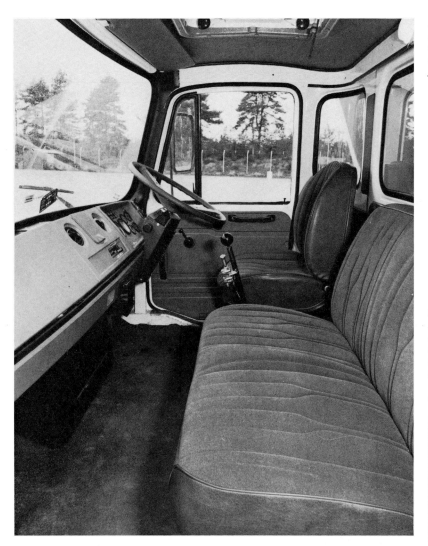

Leyland, with their conventional Landtrain cab, show what they can do. The engine is out front, hence no awkward bulge in the floor

BELOW: *Modern cooperation. This 1981 Seddon Atkinson shows British, European and American influence endorsing the impression that no manufacturer can live solely on its domestic market. Today, weight saving is the main development target*

road, A3 to the Portsmouth road, A4 to the Great West or Bath road, A5 to Telford's Watling Street running right through to Holyhead on the Isle of Anglesey, A6 to the somewhat meandering route that eventually reaches Carlisle. From there, the road to Edinburgh was dubbed A7, the one linking Scottish capital with Glasgow became A8, whilst A9 was given to the road that took over where the Great North Road left off and itself ended at the coastal town of Wick.

The eventual trunk road network included many more routes than these and the ones linking the big industrial conurbations naturally carried the heaviest burden of commercial traffic. Needless to say, the Ministry of Transport did not immediately pour money into fitting the new trunk routes for the traffic. Generally they were narrow, winding ways that made the heavy truck driver's task a difficult one. Loaded truck power-to-weight ratios were abysmally low and made climbing even the gentlest gradient a painfully slow process. Once down into bottom gear, it

The modern cab must soothe the driver yet not inhibit him. This Daf 2800 interior shows the Dutch sleeper cab

tended to be arguable whether or not the wheels were visibly turning and there was no chance of gearing up until almost level ground was reached. Downhill progress had to be almost as leisurely in order to conserve brakes which were liable to fade under any sort of prolonged application, so the lowest gears had to be selected to secure maximum braking effort from the engine. Under these conditions, even the truck's best friends could not deny that it was truly a mobile road block. Even so, on many of the night runs somewhat amazing average speeds were achieved, and often expected by aggressive operators; the already archaic speed limit of 20 mph was far from being on the way out and there was every reason to treat it with contempt. Not that speeding(!) truck drivers could expect any mercy from the police. The ridiculous limit made it all to easy to trap a few when things were quiet on the crime front. This situation was to persist for little short of two more decades!

Meanwhile, the two European dictators, Hitler in Germany and Mussolini in Italy, had decreed the construction of strategic networks of special motor roads. Ostensibly, the new roads were to be designed for high speed travel unimpeded by intersections, sharp bends or steep gradients. In its reporting, the media of the day made a very great deal of the race track image which was so easy to promote. German racing cars were, in fact, let loose on a stretch of new autobahn to attack a few world speed records, one of the very many ploys by which Hitler aimed to boost national prestige. Mussolini only managed to have constructed some short lengths of single carriageway autostrada serving tourist rather than commercial routes. There is no doubt that, with the firm intention of making war in mind, the two dictators were fully aware of the potential military value of the new roads. It does seem doubtful, however, that they envisaged them as the commercial life-lines they were to become. In the event, the military potential was never realised, probably because the Rome-Berlin Axis powers had to fight the war hampered by a chronic shortage of oil. If the pattern of hostilities had been only slightly changed, the story might have been different.

In the light of the incredibly sluggish pre-war performance of Britain's road planners and builders, it may seem very hard to believe that Hitler and Mussolini were not on their own in planning for new roads. By the time war came a surprising number of ordinary British people seemed to be aware that they happened to be living on the line of a proposed new road. With a war to win, few of them could believe that the phantom carriageways would ever materialise. With the war over, it still seemed that the plans would never emerge from the back rooms where they were conceived. Those people who lived long enough to see the motorways finally coming into existence were doubly surprised to find how accurate many of the pre-war tidings and rumours of roads to come had been. The time lapse between the rumours and the reality was anything from twenty to thirty years according to which motorway was involved.

During all those years, in war and peace British trucks had to lumber on over totally inadequate roads, their long-suffering drivers having to be thankful for any improvements, however minor, that made travelling the trunk routes just a little less of an ordeal. On the busiest sections, such as that part of the A5 serving as the main road link between London and the industrial West Midlands, rapidly increasing congestion often wiped out any gains as soon as or before the work was completed. Arduous routes like the one followed by the A6 from the capital to the north west remained simply arduous. Much of the immediately pre-war expenditure on road improvements had gone into making the private motorist's lot a better one. So the week-end drivers were the real beneficiaries as most of the new works involved easing the routes from the big towns and cities to the coastal resorts. As ever, the needs of commercial traffic were given scant attention.

The defeated nations ordered things differently. Both Italy and Germany rapidly built on to their pre-war systems and before this country opened its very first motorway they had gone a very long way towards the completion of comprehensive national networks. Logically enough, the development of trucks capable of using these networks to the best advantage was off to a flying start while British makers staggered on with all their design parameters decided in the context of the 20 mph speed limit.

3 Nationalisation versus the private sector

State take-over . . . nationalisation sets a trend . . . private sector re-formed . . . pie in the sky . . . first motorway . . . European schemes . . . more pie in the sky . . . A5 agony . . . HGV speed limits raised . . . and lowered . . . plating arrives . . . six bhp per ton . . . then the first fuel crisis.

1948 and post war recovery. The United Dairies Bedford artic is a pre-war model of 3 tons. At the time these trucks undertook bulk delivery, local deliveries were still done by horse drawn vehicles

Victory for the Allies in World War II did not seem to change things very much on the British home front. Wartime austerity was still rife in the land despite the brave words of the politicians. The victory of more apparent consequence to the transport industry was that of the Labour Party in the first postwar general election. Although few of the ordinary voters fully realised it, the new government had committed itself to an intensive programme of nationalisation. Little time was lost in implementing this, and in 1947 the Transport Act that set up the British Transport Commission was passed through Parliment. The Commission's brief was 'to provide, secure or promote the provision of an adequate, economical and properly integrated system of public inland transport and port facilities within Great Britain, and to extend and improve that system.' Brave words, indeed, and there were many more to follow but precious little in the way of original ideas or action.

1949 Bedford rigid operated by British Road Services through J. J. Thody Transport (BTC) Ltd. The truck is brand new

Rare Bristol 8 wheeler of 15 tons sits ready for off in 1957. Drabness does nothing for the road haulage industry. Cab styling does not have the charm of . . .

More specifically, the BTC was given the duty of acquiring certain types of road haulage concerns. Acquisition was made only of haulage firms primarily involved in the long distance carriage of goods for hire or reward. Long distance traffic was defined as 'traffic carried more than 40 miles in one or more vehicles, one or more of which was at some time more than 25 miles from its operating centre.' Certain specialised traffic was not affected—bulk carriage of liquids in tankers, furniture removals, meat and livestock transport, abnormal indivisible loads. It says a great deal for the resilience of the road transport set-up that it was to manage to survive having this dog's dinner of a measure rammed down its throat.

So in due course the non-specialised hauliers were dispossessed and their vehicles began to be operated by the state owned British Road Services. The period of nationalisation lasted until 1953 when the first Conservative government since the war unscrambled the 1947 legislation. A disposals board was set up to supervise the sale of 35,000 BRS vehicles. The state haulier was allowed to stay in business and with about 16,000 vehicles on the road continued to function in competition with the re-formed private sector.

Nationalisation had, however, set a trend towards the establishment of bigger units which finally resulted in the formation of the Transport Development Group, a huge conglomerate of medium-sized haulage undertakings. Development was the key word and the Group was able to provide the sort of finance that had always been lacking when it became clear that a road transport operation had to involve more than just driving and servicing the simplest of trucks. The time was also ripe for the expansion of own-account operations, many big manufacturing firms building up large fleets to carry their own goods and running them as independent transport concerns. Despite all this rationalisation of the industry, the traditional pattern involving very many one-man and family businesses persisted and still persists. There are still in existence numerous small hauliers running only one, two or three vehicles, in fact about half of the 150,000 licensed haulage operations are run by owner-drivers.

. . . this 1950 Maudslay Maharajah, also in BRS livery. Single fog lamps appeared to be mandatory, but their effectiveness was debatable

Since the re-establishment of the private sector, it has been allowed to carry on relatively unmolested by governments, although a new system of regulation and licensing was imposed in 1968. 'Quality Licensing' was the name of the game and, quite reasonably, the legislation required an applicant for a licence to demonstrate his/her fitness to run and maintain a haulage fleet. Interference by doctrinaire politicians now centred on schemes designed to integrate fully the state road and rail freight services. Quantity Licensing was the weapon used to enable the newly-formed National Freight Corporation to serve as the spearhead for integration.

The latter is, of course, simply a euphemism for the transfer of freight from road to rail. Relatively recent entrants into this age old arena are the environmentalists, in one guise or another, some of whom seem to believe that the long retreat of rail before road can somehow be easily reversed. They fail to see that the truck is now the most important single element in the apparatus of modern living. Its battle with the railways has become a non-contest; it never was all that fierce a fight as it was simply one

BELOW: *European regulations favoured the draw bar trailer in the 1950s and 1960s, while the UK was going the artic way. This late 1950s' Daf shows little real development from the pre-war days*

ABOVE: *European artic of the mid-1950s. Büssing tanker looks remarkably undated*

FAR TOP LEFT: *Modern styling for BRS in 1978 is this side curtained articulated trailer available for rent*

TOP LEFT: *This is a heavyweight dump truck of 1951, a Commer Superpoise. Gross vehicle weight was 19,500 lb*

between relative efficiencies, and efficiency was never a strong point of the railway concept, embodying as it did the far from subtle philosophy of always insisting on using a sledge hammer to crack a nut. In the context of road/rail rivalry, efficiency must be measured by the degree of success achieved in satisfying the needs of the customer and the figures illustrating annual freight movement in Britain are as good a yardstick as any by which to judge how decisive has been the victory of the truck. During a typical year, in this case 1979, 1800 million tonnes of freight were moved. No less than 85 per cent of this was transported by road. The railways carried only a meagre 170 million tonnes.

Naturally, some of the credit for this overwhelming victory must be given to the fairly successful, if very tardy, postwar implementation of the long pigeon-holed plans to provide Britain with an adequate road system. As early as 1946 the Ministry of Transport had announced what seemed like a commendably positive policy aimed at putting the antiquated, war-neglected network to rights. Like so many similar previous statements it was to turn out to have been wildly optimistic mainly because no-one seemed to have any very clear idea as to where the money was going to come from. The Road Fund had not yet been abolished (this was not to happen until 1955) but expenditure on the roads bore no relationship to the amount of cash collected in licence fees and fuel tax. Expenditure always failed to match receipts by a considerable margin.

Hope springs eternal, though, and even the most cynically minded road users could not help being dazzled by the prospect of the published 10 year programme in which the first two years were to be employed in the restoration of regular maintenance work to an acceptable level and the beginning of new works of so-called first priority. The succeeding three years were to see increased (?) activity on major road works including a limited number of motorways serving the development areas. Finally, five(!) years were to be spent on the comprehensive reconstruction of the principal national routes including a further number of motorways.

The above exclamation mark is fully justified by what happened next. Beginning in 1948, the next five years witnessed a massive reduction in the amounts spent annually on every aspect of the road network. Expenditure on maintenance and minor improvements declined by 34 per cent in real terms compared with the average spending on these from 1936–9. That on major improvements and new construction was down by almost 80 per cent. Hope apparently also springs eternal in the politician's breast. In 1949 when there was obviously not a hope in hell of British trucks being able to travel on a British motorway for ten, perhaps twenty more years, a Special Roads Act was passed which recognised the principal of motorways and special purpose roads reserved exclusively for particular classes of traffic. The Act also provided the necessary enabling powers for their construction and, believe it or not, before the end of the year the first order was made dealing with 27 miles of the South Wales, Bristol and Birmingham motorway system. That was a very prime piece of pie in the sky. A full nine years later eight miles of substandard motorway were opened. It constituted the Preston by-pass which it was planned to incorporate eventually into M6, the projected six lane link between Birmingham and Carlisle. The new by-pass had only four lanes and was thus going to have to be rebuilt within a very few years of its opening.

The year 1949 was also the one when pie in the sky was being cooked on a substantial scale on the recently war-ravished continent of Europe. In contrast to relatively unscathed Britain, the countries of western Europe had emerged from the war with railway systems that had suffered almost total destruction. In some areas their roads had fared only a little

Rare 1957 tractor from Alfa Romeo known as the Tipo 1000. *Wheelbase of this tractor appears quite long by modern standards*

better. Nevertheless, continental truck operators were not slow in recognising that their big break had arrived. the International Road Transport Union was formed in Geneva in 1948 to further the cause of road transport. The next year a conference held in the Swiss lakeside city began to discuss the development of a network of international main traffic arteries. The expressed intention was the creation of 26,000 miles of standard pattern roads; included in this grand plan were ambitious schemes for the boring of road tunnels under the Alps, notably one through the heart of Europe's highest mountain, Mont Blanc. Simultaneously another conference in Geneva was considering construction and use regulations designed to achieve some sort of uniformity in the vehicles destined to traverse the new road system. Proposed maximum dimensions and weights were greater than those then legal in Britain and British makers keen to export to Europe were not able to make much headway. Continental truckers were asking for more power and more sophisticated transmissions than were on offer in British on-highway trucks. The story was different in the traditional UK export markets where smooth roads or roads at all were a rarity. Business was booming to the extent that Britain was on the way to becoming the world's main exporter of commercial vehicles.

At long last a significant length of motorway was opened, somewhat to the surprise of most British road users. The 87 miles of the six laned M1 plus the four laned M45 opened a completely new route between London and Birmingham. Until then the majority of the vast army of trucks plying between the metropolis and the industrial Midlands had used the

More typical Italian truck of mid-1950s through to, say, 1963 was this Fiat 682 N2. Many such vehicles made in Italy wore right hand drive even for domestic use. Familiar cast steel wheels are fitted

A5 (the Romans' Watling Street) and the A45, and year by year the road originally laid down by the Romans had become more and more clogged with heavies. Not until a couple of years before the M1 opened was the HGV speed limit raised from 20 mph to 30 mph, and, as the pulse of peacetime manufacturing industry quickened, all through the fifties seemingly endless crocodiles of trucks crept slowly both northwards and southwards along the A5 by day and by night. It was fortunate that much of this overburdened trunk route to the Midlands was through easy terrain. There were, however, some longish undulations scattered along its length which were capable of severely taxing the strength of under-powered and/or overloaded vehicles. Even the well-maintained, correctly loaded trucks of the day were short on power, disposing of nothing like sufficient bhp per ton to be capable of recovering readily from the fairly frequent baulking suffered on the far from severe upgrades. Momentum was at such a premium that too often the road would be blocked completely as one truck overtook another with agonising slowness, the two of them sometimes fully occupying a narrow village street, their loads overhanging the kerbs intended to guard skinny footpaths, their thundering diesels shuddering the windows and walls of the little houses that seemed to cringe visibly as the often smoking exhausts played a parallel duet. Despite incidents like this, the accident rate was not particularly high, A5 never earned the reputation of being a killer road like at least one of the overloaded truck routes in Europe today. The hall-mark of the safe driver is his ability to adapt to the existing road conditions, and the truckers on the trunk routes in the main were as worthy of wearing this stamp of quality as any piece of pure gold.

It was the heyday of the lamp signalling code, which then was as effective in promoting the maximum use of limited road space as it was in endowing truck driving with a mystique much admired by those drivers of lesser vehicles who were bright enough to appreciate its value. The

Single screen cabovers are now almost standard. Aerodynamics are still largely ignored by manufacturers – there is still a long way to go before light weight and smooth shapes contribute to increased fuel efficiency

code was used mainly to assist overtaking, a manoeuvre often resented by overtaken car drivers. Not so the truck driver who gives all the help he can to get one long load safely past another. He knows just how difficult it is to judge exactly where his distant tailboard is, so the overtaker is advised when it is safe to pull in front of the overtaken truck by a flash from its headlamps. When the new leader is safely back in the nearside lane, a flash from his tail-lamps signals his thanks. Since the car makers began to fit headlamp flashing equipment in all their products, the indiscriminate flashing of lamps by all and sundry has diminished the value of the once invaluable code.

But though no one had yet called them 'Juggernauts', those were dark days for the long haul truck. Its capacity for transporting heavy loads economically from door to door was ever more and more in demand although the roads necessary to enable it to satisfy that demand had been too long in coming. The truckers then travelling the A5 knew vaguely that massive construction works were going on just to the east of the agony road, but it is doubtful if many of them appreciated how much their world would change once the works were completed. Meanwhile there was little they could do to ease the round-the-clock purgatory being suffered by villages such as Redbourn, Markyate and Little Brickhill, names that mean nothing to their successors cruising easily down the motorway.

Predictably, perhaps, when the M1/M45 London–Birmingham route was finally opened many truck drivers were quick to assert quite forcibly that they had no intention of using it. To them the old familiar route with its equally familiar rest and refuelling places made up the work environment they knew best. The pace may have been slow, often painfully slow, nevertheless it was one they had had to get used to. The new motorway was to them very much an unknown quantity, imagination suggesting that it was an arid, featureless tarmac and

The European truck is losing individuality. Here a Daf 2300 leads a 2800 leads a Guy. Such are the vehicle construction regulations that individual interpretations are limited. Cost efficiency is important too

concrete desert bereft of all the usual and useful landmarks, a speedway where the pace was going to be killing in more ways than one. Driver-resistance to using the new motorway was, however, to be very short-lived. Soon the old route had become relatively deserted, the A5 section in particular reverting to being a quiet country road affording a pleasant drive for the few truckers who stayed with it. Not long afterwards they were dismayed to find that most of their favourite roadside food and fuel establishments had been forced to close down. This pattern was to be repeated all over the country as each new motorway was brought into service . . . along the A4 with the opening of M4, along the A6 when M6 was completed, along the A38 as M5 crept ever farther down to the south west. As time went on, the motorways collected traffic from far beyond the immediately parallel routes until in certain regions congestion began once again to impede the progress of the long haul truck, but making comparisons with road conditions of the pre-motorway days is far from comparing like with like.

Considering how restrictive had been the speed limits applied to HGVs ever since the beginning of the motor age, it was very surprising that initially no motorway limit was imposed. For fully two years it was theoretically possible for 24 tons of aggressive truck to thunder quite legally down the M-ways at 100 mph or more. In practice, however, the home-built HGV of the early years was strictly a slow lane vehicle, able to trundle along at 40 to 50 mph with slightly more to come when circumstances happened to be favourable. In 1962 an overall motorway limit of 70 mph was imposed, but of more interest and more relevance to trucking at the time was the raising of the limit for heavy trucks travelling on all-purpose roads from 30 mph to 40 mph. By the time the latter half of the sixties had arrived, private motorists with a passion for hogging the middle lanes of the three lane motorways were being made aware that big

Bulk tanker hauled by Dutch registered Scania 111. Three axle trailer spreads the load, at least according to some theorists. Bulk liquids and powders are efficiently carried this way although care is needed

trucks capable of cruising on the level at 60 mph had been let loose and were increasing in number. Their drivers, banned from using the outside lane, were not amused to find themselves effectively barred from overtaking since the obstructive motorists were often little more than keeping pace with the trucks in the nearside lane. The same situation is not unknown today.

Then in 1972 something of a landmark was reached when legislation concerned with keeping speeds up rather than down was placed on the statute book. The new law specified that all new HGVs had to be designed to have a power-to-weight ratio of at least six bhp per ton. This meant that top weight artics grossing 32 tons needed just under 200 bhp to stay legal, scarcely sufficient muscle to provide a dazzling performance both uphill and down dale but definitely step in the right direction. It seemed that authority was at last beginning to shed the lingering remains of the red flag mentality. It should not be forgotten, though, that the spreading of motorways and the conversion of many all-purpose roads to dual carriageways had made this legislation less important than it would have been in the days when the frustrated crocodiles clogged the old trunk routes.

Somewhat ironically, the minimum power-to-weight regulation had been slightly preceded by the lowering of the motorway speed limit for HGVs to 60 mph. This was presumably regarded as a safety measure, but for the majority of trucks the figure was a somewhat academic one as long as their drivers were given the same latitude the private motorist seems to enjoy. Other legislation, apparently mainly concerned with safety, had brought in the plating system under which a maximum authorised laden weight was determined and then marked on the vehicle. Important though these measures were, they paled into insignificance when rumours of possible fuel shortages began to circulate. Until then the automotive world seems to have given little or no credence to the concept of a world without oil, building more and more wasteful vehicles at an ever-increasing rate. The truck makers were better than most, mainly because the fiercely competitive road transport industry has always been acutely sensitive to fuel costs. As rumour hardened into fact and the service area derv tanks began to run dry, whole nations held their breaths and took time off to consider how dependent was the whole fabric of their societies on oil both as a fuel and as a raw material. Truckers dependent on roadside supplies ran under the constant threat of being stranded, and found quite frightening the stark fact that the continuance of trucking relied entirely on an uninterrupted flow of oil. Equally disturbing was the glaring absence in the long term of any sort of alternative likely to be capable of keeping afloat the tottering edifice called civilisation. A few voices were briefly heard advocating that the waning supplies of oil should be conserved for use primarily as transport fuel, a call which predictably went completely unheeded. Fortunately, the fuel famine eased quite quickly and everything was apparently soon restored to normal. Most people looking back on those significant days would now be prepared to acknowledge that it was just as well that the warning came when it did.

4 Hail the Juggernaut

Writing on the wall . . . time versus fuel . . . turbo take-over . . . despeeding shows results . . . punching a truck-sized hole . . . slippery shapes wanted . . . hiding the unattractive bits . . . a thundering Juggernaut . . . staggering gains . . . tonnes to tons.

After the 1973 fuel crisis and the emergence of the Middle Eastern petroleum exporting countries as a world political force, nothing could ever be quite the same again on the trunk routes of Britain. When finally derv had begun to flow reasonably freely from the pumps again, a certain amount of complacency soon crept back into both the manufacturing and the operating industry, only to be rather brutally checked by the apparently endless succession of fuel price rises. Those operators who had seen the writing on the wall from the first were joined by those whose attention was finally captured by rocketing fuel bills. There was no mistaking the message now, economise or die, it said. Making the most of every gallon of derv was not now simply a way of maximising profits, it was the only way to survive.

To give the inter-war truck makers and users their due, they had been very quick to take advantage of the overwhelming superiority of the diesel over the petrol engine in the matter of efficiency, and hence in the economical use of fuel. But the diesel revolution of the thirties had been strictly a one off; even now, almost fifty years on, there is nothing on or just below the horizon which is likely to bring about an improvement in efficiency to match what happened then. Since those days, engine designers and builders have worked wonders in the way of squeezing more and more energy from every gallon, though they must be acutely aware of how their efforts can be, and often are, wholly neutralised by operators and drivers who count time-saving as more important than fuel saving.

Government attempts to make the available fuel go further were first focused on the imposition of a blanket speed limit of 50 mph, but this turned out to be too simple an approach and was eventually abandoned. As far as truck operation was concerned, the new limit was irrelevant except on motorways. In any case, on occasion the time factor can be the more important one when it comes to measuring a straight profit or loss. When fuel was relatively cheap, time saving was always the most important factor in the eyes of very many operators. Faced with the sort of fierce competition which was and is far from being unknown in the transport world, drivers would more likely be offered a bonus on tonnage moved than on diesel saved. However, any fuel saved probably

ABOVE: *Famous Rolls-Royce Eagle engine. Compact and powerful six cylinder diesel, with the bonus of a special name*

ABOVE RIGHT: *Turbo charged Daf DKSE diesel engine with intercooler. Daf uses turbo name plate on the front of the truck*

RIGHT: *American based Cummins VT 504 used by Foden – 8.3 litre turbo V8*

FAR RIGHT: *Cummins Big Cam E400 engine, designed in America, built in Scotland. 14 litres and 400 bhp gross*

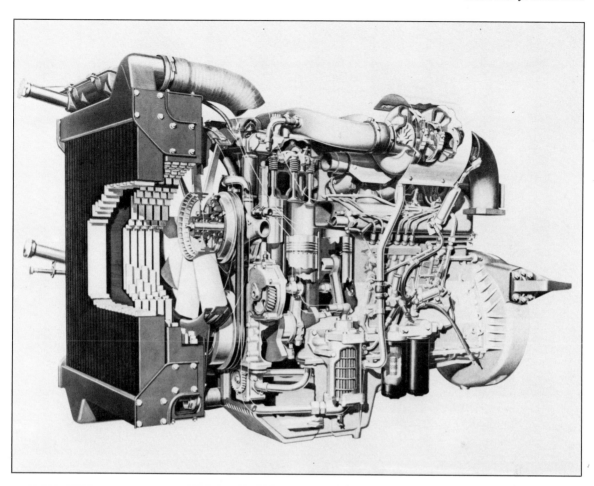

RIGHT: *The rigid truck won't disappear. Ford have been the postwar master of the medium to heavyweight variety. The old Thames Trader was curiously styled but a winner in every way*

represented only part of the savings a driver skilled in economy could achieve. When the scheduling complications involved in trying to make best use of the hours a driver is permitted to work have to be taken into account, together with the possible savings in tyre, brake and mechanical wear and tear, it seems unlikely that the average small operator would ever be able to get his sums right. The bigger ones, who these days could call in the aid of a computer, might then be able to make a better stab at it, but, even so, the utterly unpredictable and constantly changing conditions encountered on the road can upset the most carefully prepared of schedules.

Where traffic concentrations are low and conditions that much more predictable, computer technology may provide a complete answer. The National Swedish Road and Traffic Research Institute has worked out methods and computer programmes for calculating the transport time and fuel consumption for vehicles in simulated service, and applied the results to long distance services on two typical Swedish trunk roads. Going to these lengths, of course, still gets completely nowhere unless the man at the wheel cooperates absolutely. The Swedish technologists do try to get the upperhand in the end, though, by gearing vehicle design to the computer findings, so that the maximum economy is achieved when the driver is following his natural inclinations, or, more likely in a country like Sweden, he is driving the way he has been trained to do.

There can be no denying that Swedish technology has had a very considerable influence on modern truck design. As long ago as 1954 one of the two very successful Swedish truck makers, Volvo, was producing a range of turbocharged diesels when most other manufacturers were still putting their faith in naturally aspirated engines. Pressuring the air into the combustion chambers is a sure way of increasing the power output of virtually any internal combustion engine. When a positively driven blower is used to help charge the cylinders it is known as a supercharger. A turbocharger is simply a supercharger driven by a turbine propelled by the exhaust gases impinging on its rotor. Not every automobile engineer believes that turbocharging is the best way of using the forced induction principle. Swiss engineers have been experimenting for several years with a system which transfers pressure energy directly from the exhaust gas to the intake air. Simple turbocharging is, however, an elegant way of doing this because the engine designer does not have to provide for some sort of mechanical drive as he would have for a conventional blower, nor is he tied too rigidly as to where he has to locate the turbocharger. In service the latter does fall down somewhat by being unable to provide an instant response to the opening of the throttle. Boost build-up is initially relatively slow as the turbine has to be accelerated to very high revs before anything much happens, which is why normal aspiration is often favoured for engines engaged in mainly stop-start work.

The original Volvo approach was to use turbocharging to extract high power outputs from relatively small engines and success in this was achieved while at the same time commendable economy and refinement were wedded to excellent reliability, no mean achievment. Some other makers were not so successful and for a time turbocharging was thought

ABOVE: *Couldn't be uglier. Model 56 GSF ERF rigid of 1960 ran 18½ tons GVW. Early use of a part fibreglass cab. Gardner provided the power*

by some to be synonymous with doubtful reliability. No-one now has any reason for believing this and, in addition, the turbocharger has continued to gain new friends due to its ability to help clean up exhaust emissions.

The continuing search for better and better fuel economy has led other designers in the direction of low crankshaft speeds and high cubic capacities. In the forefront of these developments has been the Mark III Eagle diesel built by Rolls-Royce. This is an in-line six cylinder turbocharged unit of 12 litres capacity designed with weight-saving in mind. When a German truck builder adopted the advertising slogan: 'What we want are fewer revolutions and more torque', Rolls-Royce had already succeeded in going along this road with the L series, managing to lower the speed at which maximum power was produced from 2100 revs to 1900 revs. Power output remained the same. Besides improvements in fuel economy, the gains included less noise, a potentially longer life and lower maintenance costs.

Meanwhile, the multi-national Cummins Engine Co. had been working on roughly parallel lines. Again the basic powerplant was a big turbocharged in-line six, this time of 14 litres cubic capacity. Again the technique was to despeed the economy engine so that maximum power was developed at only 1900 rpm. The resulting E series was claimed to be 10 per cent more economical than its predecessors. Built at Shotts in

Twenty year old articulated truck from Leyland as Britain was 'going that way'. Beaver cab and Scammell trailer from 1960. That cab style was used with many brand and model names. Trailer was 25 feet 9 inches long

Scotland, Cummins 14 litre diesels power many of the premium trucks built in Britain.

The truck manufacturers have their part to play in any economy drive mounted by the engine builders. It is up to them to engineer their drive lines to match the characteristics of the engines they fit. Then, inevitably, it is back to the driver again. Cummins point out in their advice on driving the E series that the best returns come from making full use of the low engine speeds, indicating how a 32 ton tractor and 13 ft high van semi-trailer could cruise at 60 mph with the engine turning over at only 1700 rpm. At that speed the Cummins E290 would be producing 200 bhp from the 282 available. Should the driver decide to press on at the maximum governed speed of 66 mph, this 10 per cent increase in road speed with the engine now up to 1900 revs, would incur a fuel penalty of as much as 25 per cent.

It should be explained here that engine characteristics play only a small part in this. The major contributor to an increase in fuel consumption under these conditions is the atmosphere itself. Power absorbed by the resistance of the air to having a truck-sized hole punched through it varies according to the cube of the speed, and thus a relatively small increase in road speed demands a relatively enormous increase in power and a corresponding decrease in mpg results.

RIGHT: *Albion Chieftain Super Six tractor with 25 feet Scammell semi-trailer. Date 1963. Compare with Leyland cab opposite*

LEFT: *From Europe came trucks like this Scania-Vabis LBS 7642 also of 1963. Refrigerated semi-trailers were used extensively there before they came to Britain*

About half of the engine's power output at normal cruising speeds goes into overcoming rolling resistance, the other half being used to counter air drag. The average truck constitutes something of an aerodynamic disaster so there seems to be plenty of scope for improvement in this area. There is no way of avoiding the displacement of about 20 tons of the atmosphere during each mile covered, which is the weight a tractor hauling a van semi-trailer has to push aside. But something can be done about how it is displaced. If the air can be persuaded to flow more easily over the external surfaces of the tractor and trailer, drag can be reduced proportionately. The secret is to prevent the air flow from separating from these surfaces, not an easy task considering the angular nature of much truck hardware. The latest cabs, like the one designed for the Leyland T45, show considerable gains in aerodynamic efficiency though these cannot be of too much account if the trailer remains simply a square-cornered box. In the long term, truck designers may be able to come up with a slippery shape that is practical as well as efficient. It will undoubtedly have to include fairings which cover the gap between tractor and trailer as well as skirts closing in the running gear. Highly desirable also would be some sort of undershield. On some types of work, none of these may turn out to be too vulnerable to damage or obstructive during maintenance operations: it is pretty certain, however, that in many instances they will prove impossibly difficult to work with even to the point of making coupling and uncoupling a lengthy chore. In the short term there are economies to be gained by relatively simple measures like rounding the front corners of van trailers, fitting them with shallow nose cones, grafting deflectors on to the cab top to intercept and smooth the air flow over the trailer.

Streamlined trucks already exist, serving as aids to designers seeking their next step forward. It may be that the cost-effectiveness of slippery-sided vehicles will not justify making a really big switchover. Yet there must be something to be said for the cosmetic benefits which undoubtedly ensue. Because of the tireless attacks mounted by the environmental lobby, the industry definitely needs trucks that arouse admiration rather than fear and resentment. So there is much to be said for hiding the unattractive parts of the truck's anatomy, at the same time improving under-run protection both at the sides and to the rear and creating smooth surfaces that stay clean or at least justify any effort put into cleaning them. Very much a signal failure as a fuel saver or performance enhancer, yet achieving a quite striking cosmetic success, the inter-war introduction of streamlined steam locomotives on the railways must hold some lessons for the road transport industry. Whether by accident or design, the latest tractor cabs with any claims to being aerodynamically effective also tend to have lost the aggressive look which was very typical of some of the previous models. This must be counted as a partial step, at least, towards the much needed creation of a better image for the truck in the eyes of the public.

Every motorist must by now be aware of how important the behaviour of his right foot is in determining how far a gallon will take him. His fellow driver at the wheel of a 32 ton truck has rather less freedom to

Italy was slow with the artic. Once again they stuck with the draw bar trailer. This Fiat has a high all-up weight, however. Made in the mid 1960s this one was caught by the camera in 1972. Note right-hand drive

There is still a wide variance between the British standard and that used on the Continent. There's a considerable difference in length between these two semi-trailers, seen here parked at Dover. The three axle trailer uses only single wheels each side. European tractor has longer wheelbase

engage in serious fuel wasting by over-revving, as his diesel engine is governed to prevent the crankshaft speed rising to the realms where total inefficiency rules. An impatient trucker, however, has plenty of opportunity to be profligate of fuel if his truck happens to be geared for high speeds. Then fast running in top gear will be possible without exceeding the crankshaft's governed speed except, perhaps, on downhill stretches where engine revs may soar somewhat beyond the set limit. A truck governed to 70 mph could then run up to 75 mph and all the time the air it is having to push out of the way is, in effect, becoming more of a solid wall. Dropping its speed to 60 mph should effect a dramatic drop in fuel demand. One way of ensuring that the more economical speed is adhered to is to fit a road speed limiter, and these are finding more and more favour with operators as derv prices climb to ever dizzier heights. The device is already used for obvious reasons on many vehicles carrying dangerous loads. Apart from lengthening the life of any truck, a road

speed governor offers the worth-while spin-off of lessening its impact on the environment. While the arguments rage about the desirability or otherwise of raising permissible gross weights, the speed factor tends to be forgotten. Without stressing what must to some extent be the indeterminate effect of speed on road surface wear and tear, the case for reasonable speed limitation stands up well on the noise element alone. A truck running easily at 60 mph generates a considerable volume of sound, but speed it up by 25 per cent and it becomes no more, no less than a thundering Juggernaut which can quite easily persuade a tolerant public to become intolerant.

At the present time various factions hostile to transport efficiency are trying to persuade the public that trucks carrying heavier loads than is now permissible would be a very real menace to the well-being of the environment. The truth is, however, that the main impact of increasing maximum permissible gross weights would fall on the oil companies. A saving of something like 18 per cent in derv consumption is the probable outcome of pushing up maximum weights from 32 to 44 tons, so there is no doubt about which of the suggested oil conservation measures leads the field. Additional economies would result from aspects such as driver productivity, lower overall fleet mileages and so on, as illustrated by the somewhat staggering gains in efficiency consequent on the raising of gross operating weights from 24 to 32 tons in 1964. Then the cost of carrying freight sank back to pre-war levels!

The arguments against heavier trucks were recently thrown many (about 2000) times at a committee chaired by Sir Arthur Armitage, a university professor who has never given the faintest hint of being a truck-lover. Like all committees, this one was extremely productive of paper, its report running to 159 pages. But it also demonstrated a commendably brave honesty in deciding that there was no feasible

ABOVE LEFT: *Foden Fleetmaster S10 with refrigerated semi-trailer. No aerodynamic aid, perhaps, because the Petter fridge unit needs cool air*

ABOVE: *Second Fleetmaster with curtain side semi sports cab mounted spoiler. This truck has a Cummins diesel*

ABOVE RIGHT: *An attempt at streamlining. Special moulding has been fitted to the semi. Efficiency is debatable*

BELOW: *Clever streamlining shows careful thought. Expensive construction shown here should achieve considerable savings in fuel. Note how the underside of the bumper has been faired in on the Ford Transcontinental*

alternative to road transport. Even braver was the decision to recommend the increasing of the maximum permitted gross weight to 44 tonnes, a move calculated to save the country up to £230 million a year. Judging by present buying trends, the legalising of the 44 tonne artic would persuade about 75 per cent of the operators now running 32 tonners to take advantage of the new law, though few of them are convinced that such a big increase in the top weight will ever be sanctioned by Parliament. Actually the proposed weight in traditional English measure amounts to only 43 tons, as the tonne is slightly less than a ton. At present there are very many 32 ton trucks registered in this country which were intended by their designers to run at higher weights. Most of them consist of a two-axled tractor hauling a two-axled semi-trailer, and Armitage suggested that these should be allowed to load up to a gross weight of 34 tonnes. This means that operators who bought tractors with high design weights in anticipation of these being legalised will lose out unless they can always couple their tractors to tri-axled semi-trailers, in which case Armitage would allow them to load up to 38 tonnes. But those who wish to take advantage of the top weight proposed by Armitage will have to buy three-axled tractors and always couple them to tri-axled semi-trailers. Those few operators who run draw-bar combinations will have to comply with a similar multiplication of axles. Thus the full implementation of Armitage would mean a general reduction in axle weights and a subsequent reduction in road and bridge damage.

The Armitage committee flatly refused to sanction any increase in maximum overall dimensions apart from allowing a token 0.5 metre increase of the 15 metre maximum artic length, ostensibly to cater for the fitting of slightly bigger cabs. So it looks as if the trucks on general haulage duties in Britain are not going to be allowed to grow any bigger in the foreseeable future, a disappointment for truck enthusiasts.

5 Artic revolution

Artic revolution . . . flexibility the key . . . trucks across the seas . . . TIR means ITR . . . import invasion . . . looking after the driver . . . ahead of Formula 1 . . . everything including the sink . . . useless bunks . . . committee with tongue in cheek.

The container revolution was just that. Here a Mercedes-Benz LP1624 cabover of the early 1960s is easily loaded at speed. Initial capitalisation was high

You did not have to be a particularly acute observer of the heavy transport scene during the fifties and sixties to be able to see that a revolution was in progress. To anyone with a long memory or a knowledge of industrial history, it was very reminiscent of the earliest days of the application of machine power to road haulage. Then the heavy hauls were entrusted to the steam traction engine or road locomotive which took over where the horse left off, pulling loads to their destination rather than carrying them. Later on, when load-carrying trucks had taken over the transporting of the bulk of the goods going by road, both petrol and diesel tractive units were built to take on the haulage of indivisible loads as heavy as 100 tons or more. The trailers used were of the self-contained or drawbar type and it was the eventual emergence of the semi-trailer as a popular load carrier that finally sparked off the artic revolution. Instead of simply hauling the load, the tractive units had to carry some of it rather in the manner of a horse pulling a two wheeled cart, but nevertheless were essentially tugs with no load carrying capacity of their own.

The articulated truck is virtually as old as the industry and it now dominates the haulage scene almost everywhere there is a well-developed road system. It scores over the rigid truck in several ways, and at the root of its superiority is flexibility in more senses than one. On the road its mechanical flexibility makes it remarkably manoeuvrable whilst providing a load deck as long as 40 ft, in overall use it offers the flexibility which enables tractors and semi-trailers to be exchanged according to circumstances. Thus, one tractive unit can serve almost any number of semi-trailers, or vice versa. The trailers can be loaded or unloaded whilst one of them is on the road behind the tractor; if the tractor breaks down it can be replaced by another one without the load being disturbed; a trailer can be dropped at one port, shipped across the sea to another, then picked up by a tractor over there. A particular tractor can be hitched to different types of trailer and thus operate as a tanker, refrigerated van, curtain-sided van, container carrier, bulk carrier, platform truck and so on and so on. This sort of ultra versatility is not fully exploited in every type of operation. Often advantage is taken only of on-road flexibility and the ease and speed of replacement in the event of breakdown, emergencies such as fire in the load, or when the prime mover has to be overhauled or renewed.

The artic is now the glamour truck and its appeal to the observer has as much to do with its agility as with its sheer size and power. Big though it is, there is nothing cumbersome in the way it can be threaded through the traffic or slotted into relatively minute spaces. Dynamically it is both functional and impressive to watch. Thanks to recent progress in cab design, European tractive units are more than pleasant to the eye both externally and internally. Across the Atlantic the cult of the big rig centres on conventional or bonneted tractors that, at best, can be described as brutally functional in appearance or, at worst, as being made up of incompatible bits and pieces very much in the style of the old American steam locomotive. European tractors, even when bonneted, are much more attractively styled and compare with the big yanks rather in the way the handsome, clean-limbed British railway engine out-styled its rough, tough American counterpart.

Running pretty well parallel with the artic revolution, the rapid expansion of roll-on, roll-off ferry traffic has added the glamour of long distance international and inter-continental operations to the aura of the

Tilbury and an early photograph of the specialised container ferry, Cerdic Ferry, sister ship to the Bardic Ferry. Special roll-on, roll-off facilities made this transport method grow faster than any other

Clean and efficient. Mercedes LPS1624 and container ready for international transport. Little has changed in 20 years – this is 1960

artic in Britain. Postwar Europe was the scene of a great deal of development in the field of international road haulage well before trucks from these islands were able to set wheels on continental soil, or trucks from over there could begin to roll freely along British roads. The first truck ferries were war-time tank landing craft used to convey military vehicles to and from the armed services bases in Germany. In 1956 a ship designed specifically to carry goods vehicles, the *Bardic Ferry*, began to ply between Tilbury and Antwerp. Only half a dozen years later the bulk of the traffic was made up of artics, or, rather, of semi-trailers. BRS alone were shipping more than 200 trailers each month. Specially designed tractive units were employed to shunt the trailers on and off the ship.

From then on, the number of vehicle ferries linking England with Europe multiplied with a startling rapidity. Many of them were intended to carry the ever-growing volume of private car traffic, but this was very much a seasonal demand that died almost completely during the winter. So the growth of truck traffic unaffected by the changing of the seasons became vital to the economic employment of the many ships being built. Every new ship was bigger than its predecessor and vehicle decks were laid out with trucks in mind. A major step forward came with the fitting of bow doors to enable vehicles to be driven straight through the ship. Artics no longer had to be reversed inch by inch up or down long, narrow loading ramps and ferries could be turned round more quickly. New sea routes were opened until it seemed that virtually every port on the east and south coasts of England was linked by ro-ro ferry to a corresponding port across the North Sea or the English Channel.

The nature of the traffic was changing, too, as operators began to appreciate the advantages of seeing the load through to its destination. So driver and tractor began to stay with the semi-trailer instead of handing it over to the dock shunter at the port. Thus it was that more and more

British registered trucks began to be seen running steadily over the long haul routes on the other side of the channel, while trucks bearing foreign number plates started to appear on the trunk routes and sometimes even in the little back streets of Britain. It was about then that interested observers of the road transport scene and the more curious members of the general public were beginning to wonder about the meaning of the legend 'TIR'. Most people were able to guess correctly that the white letters displayed on a blue plate had something to do with international transport operations. In fact, it simply advertised the particular truck's compliance with the requirements of a system that had been evolved to speed commercial traffic across national borders. TIR is an abbreviation of the title in French of the *Convention: Transport International des Marchandises par Route*. Translated, this means simply: Customs Convention on the International Transport of Goods by Road. This provides for the movement of goods in road vehicles across national frontiers without inspection by the Customs or the deposit of Customs Bonds. The system is wholly dependent on an approved method of applying seals to the load in such a way that anyone tampering with it would be certain to break the seals. So the TIR plate shows that the vehicle has been constructed to certain requirements which enable the sealing to be effective. For obvious reasons, the plate is normally seen only on closed vehicles, either those with rigid sides and roof or with the cargo space enclosed by an authorised design of canvas tilt. However, for journeys across the borders of the countries belonging to the European Economic Community, otherwise the Common Market, the TIR Convention has now been superseded by the Community Transit System which is also designed to facilitate the movement of goods between the EEC and Austria and Switzerland. Whichever way things are ordered,

Roll-on, roll-off and derrick loadings were possible at Tilbury. The container has few disadvantages

Two small containers for this Daf F2000 draw-bar. Whatever the size no one can deny the success of containerisation. TIR plate confirms distance this outfit has to travel

Ten year old Cummins-engined Foden with a modern bulk tanker. Some tanks were fitted into rectangular frames so that they could be treated as though they were a container and could therefore fit in with their loading and stacking arrangements

BELOW: *Heavyweight low loader from Atkinson in 1969. Three axle tractor is rare and really only suitable for abnormal loads. Cab attempts modernisation but not too successfully*

With long distances to be travelled, cabs had to be larger and more comfortable. The sleeper cab came into fashion; this is Seddon Atkinson's latest effort in 1981

BELOW: *Super sleeper cab equipment for this Renault TR305 Turbo in 1980. Roof covers TV, cooker, sink, refrigerator, air conditioning and two bunks. Known as* Le Centaure

Volvo Globetrotter cab shows similar equipment. Semi trailer features smaller diameter wheels to increase load height without creating an abnormal load. Flexible side curtaining aids loading ease

there seems to be no escape from the paperwork, and besides having to wrestle with Customs controls, the international haulier inevitably runs up against the strict regulation of the number of foreign vehicles allowed to enter various countries. As always, money has to change hands, in this case in the form of transit taxes.

The invasion of foreign registered trucks did little to conceal the fact that another influx had taken place. The longstanding supremacy of the home-built truck in this country was at last being seriously challenged. Amongst the long familiar profiles of the Leylands, Scammells, Fodens, ERFs, Atkinsons and others, there began to appear the unfamiliar outlines of trucks wearing strange-sounding names. One of these names was familiar enough to the motoring public as that worn by a Swedish car, and since then Volvo trucks have become as prominent on British roads as Volvo cars. There was a more Anglo Saxon ring about the other name, Scania, which was also Swedish, and which is now used as the sole name of a marque originally introduced here as Scania-Vabis. The Swedish pair made a formidable vanguard for the invasion and after Britain joined the Common Market it was not long before most of the European truck makers started to sell their products here. From Holland came Daf, from Germany came Man, Mercedes and Magirus Deutz, France sent Saviem and Berliet, Italy sent Fiat. Later on the Americans Mack and White arrived, though in very small numbers. Inevitably the Japanese put in an appearance with the Hino, a truck assembled in Ireland and rumoured to be scheduled to be produced over here.

So it came about that British truck manufacturers had to face the challenge from makers who were much more experienced in providing for the needs of the long haul operators simply because the latter happened to be significant customers in their own domestic market. Trucks sold on Britain's home market had always been irrevocably confined to the roads serving these islands. Therefore they had spent their working lives running over a system of smooth but narrow and

congested highways most of which crossed nothing fiercer than a gentle wold or mildly elevated moor. The longest journeys possible were short compared with many of the transcontinental trips and few British trucks were ever required to travel the total length of the land. This was a situation which had been long left behind in Europe. The Scandinavian makers had been quick to realise that in the absence of a big home market, they could raise their sales volume only by building trucks designed to appeal to the bigger European nations. Their own weight regulations were less restrictive than most, their own road conditions broadly reflected those prevailing across the continent, so they had an excellent base to work from. Volvo, in particular, took a potentially highly productive line when they decided to concentrate on designing cabs intended to persuade the drivers that what they wanted were Volvos. So looking after the driver properly was made a first priority, and this was an area where there was plenty of scope for improvement. By then the sleeper cab was no novelty in Europe and the widespread adoption of forward control was providing the man at the wheel with a commanding view of the world outside and the hazards of the road ahead. There remained the fairly intransigent problems of high noise levels, bone-shaking suspension systems and

Conventional 'short haul' sleeper cab is a common feature now for most heavyweight tractors. Strict driver schedules limit time at the wheel, hence increased popularity. This Volvo F10 has the standard cab

appalling ergonomics, all of them in part responsible for the creation of unnecessary fatigue which makes keeping control much more of a struggle than it should be. The Swedish preoccupation with safety was motive enough to sharpen the attack on such dangerous deficiencies.

Curing these ills clearly involved work centred on isolating the cab as far as possible from the machinery. Reducing the in-cab cacophony is not simply a matter of strewing around liberal amounts of sound-absorbent material. Part of the battle lies in identifying the sources of individual noises, and this can only be done with any certainty in a suitable accoustic chamber. Obviously, quietening the mechanical elements helps, while body panels and fitments made robustly assist in suppressing the demon vibrations. Cutting out the road shocks demands an equally subtle approach. In theory it should be relatively easy to suspend a heavy vehicle so that it rides smoothly over the worst road surfaces. This is because a favourable sprung to unsprung weight ratio is a major factor in making any suspension system work for, rather than against the vehicle, and a heavily laden truck cannot help but have a favourable ratio. The unsprung mass (axles, wheels, brakes and tyres) is small compared to the weight carried by the springs, which is everything else, including the load. The big snag is that the ratio changes drastically when the load is removed. Removing 20 tons or so from the back of a truck turns it into a different vehicle from the point of view of spring rates, tyre pressures etc. In practice, a truck suspension system has to provide a ride which is a reasonable compromise catering for both the laden and unladen condition, but it is normally a compromise that takes no account of the comfort and well-being of the driver. The answer then is to provide him with his own personal suspension system.

Equipping the driving seat with some sort of springing arrangement, as distinct from just a sprung cushion, is, like so many of the apparently novel things in the trucking game, far from being a new idea. Relatively recent is its refinement to the point where various springing mediums can be specified . . . torsion bar, air, steel coil and so on. Damping to cut out unnecessary bouncing is done hydraulically. Such seats are superbly comfortable, incorporating as they do a wide range of adjustments to enable drivers of varying stature to obtain their ideal driving position. The Scandinavians, egged on, perhaps, by their chilly climate, were the first to give the trucker a hot seat, the welcome warmth provided by electrical elements submerged in the upholstery. One step further in the search for the ultimate in truck-conducting environments is the provision of a suspension system for the cab itself, a very effective method of insulating the crew from road shocks and one that also helps to reduce the transmission to the cab interior of mechanical noise and vibration. There is an interesting parallel here with current racing car developments involving two separate suspension systems. Apparently a Formula 1 chassis can survive virtually without springs of any kind, and at the same time offer consequent gains in desirable handling qualities. Even world champion class drivers, however, like the rather less well paid trucker, work better when they are properly insulated from road shocks, so the day of the grand prix suspension seat and suspended monocoque cab may not be all that far away! This looks like a reversal of the claim that racing improves the breed.

Just as important a factor in the reduction of fatigue and the promotion of safety is the careful designing and locating of both the major and minor controls. Pedals angled and positioned correctly, instruments made easy to read both by day and by night, warning lights prominently and logically placed, finger tip control of lights, windscreen washers and wipers, attention to all these points has served to transform the driver's lot. Headlamp wash/wipe systems, heated mirrors, and mirror wipers are all relatively recently developed safety aids and there are certain to be more in the pipe-line.

The modern cab designer regards interior styling as an ergonomic aid, so upholstery and trim colours are carefully chosen and matched. Materials have to look good as well as being hard wearing and not soiling too easily. Inevitably, the widespread provision of bunks has led to the offering of optional equipment intended to convert the long haul tractor cab into a rather cramped motorhome of sorts. Despite the trend towards roomier and roomier cabs, most designs are short on head-room for anyone wishing to stand up, and a home providing only crouching room is no home at all. A couple of the current cabs, the Volvo Globetrotter and Ford's Transcontinental, are built high enough to make standing up and walking about more feasible, and Man is one maker now experimenting with taller cabs. With *Le Centaure*, Renault (Saviem) are obviously thinking along the same lines. The living equipment offered includes a cooker fuelled by bottled gas, refrigerator, water tank and sink, storage cupboards for food and clothes and a cab heater independent of engine heating. For climates where the cab more often needs to be cooled rather than heated, an air conditioning system can be provided. This type of equipment is clearly intended for use in countries much vaster than Britain. But even where the normal hauls are much longer than here, such equipment weighs enough to significantly reduce payloads and therefore finds favour mainly for operations involving long trips through the lesser developed countries.

For operations carried out solely in these islands, even a simple bunk in the cab is of doubtful value because little provision has been made for the safe and legal parking of trucks overnight. The average British layby is no use at all as a rest area and it is, in fact, illegal to park a truck or anything else in one for the night. The Armitage Committee (see page 60) recommended recently that the government should encourage the provision on motorway service areas of overnight lorry parking space, together with proper accommodation facilities for drivers. In going as far as to actually specify a parking fee of £10, the committee probably had its collective tongue in its collective cheek, as it must have been made fully aware of the British reluctance to allow any more precious land to be concreted or tarmacked over, a reluctance instantly transformed into total refusal by the slightest hint that trucks might be parked on it. The fatal mistake was made when this country's motorway system was designed with too few and too small parking areas, a policy far removed from that of even the smaller European countries like Belgium.

6 Semi-trailer wizardry

Takes two to make one . . . bodies to trailers . . . the fifth wheel . . . semi-trailer design constraints . . . TIR led to enclosures . . . chassisless vehicles . . . stepped frames, low loaders and tippers . . . running gear . . . variable rate suspension . . . metal and air . . . tankers and reefers.

The truck manufacturing industry has always been two-faced. Ever since the earliest days it has taken at least two separate entities to bring the whole vehicle into being, the chassis manufacturer and the body builder. Generally the latter adapted his products to fit those produced by the former, and even today body builders tend to be fabricators in the traditional materials . . . timber, plywood and sheet aluminium, with GRP (glass reinforced plastic) having been around long enough to almost warrant being ranked as 'traditional'. Latterly, the artic revolution has demanded the large scale manufacture of semi-trailers, a rather different process from the simple construction of bodies to fit on to existing chassis. The trailer maker has to construct both chassis and running gear before he can get down to the actual body building.

On this side of the Atlantic it was the British who led the way in the large scale introduction of the artic. Even as late as the second half of the nineteen-fifties the typical German autobahn 'heavy' was the drawbar

The York Prestoleg is an air operated version of the familiar landing gear. Level ground for both tractor and trailer are the only essentials for safe coupling and uncoupling

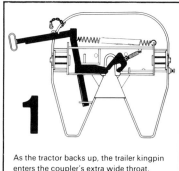

1 As the tractor backs up, the trailer kingpin enters the coupler's extra wide throat, engages the hook which pivots through 90° so that both shoulder and shank of the pin are totally enclosed around the full 360° by the hook and the coupler's jaw.

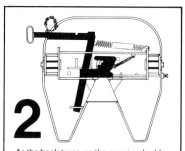

2 As the hook turns, so the massive double coil spring draws the steel wedge lock home automatically across the jaw. Thus the kingpin pulls against the solid steel wedge, which forms a 'bridge' across the coupler's throat in transit. The release handle locks on to the coupler top plate and unlocking is prevented by a safety clip.

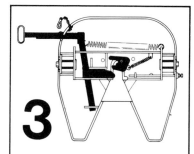

3 To release the kingpin the spring-loaded single-release handle is pulled out and secured on the notch. The hook is now free to pivot releasing the pin – leaving the coupler cocked ready to re-couple, with the handle free of notch ready to re-lock automatically.

oufit, capable of running at 60 mph plus on down grades but slowed to about 0.5 mph by the slightest rise. A similar state of affairs applied on the Italian autostrade, though here speeds tended to be low both uphill and down. On French roads there were few long haul trucks of any kind to be seen and the artic was virtually non-existent. Today the situation is very different with the roads of Europe dominated by semi-trailers carrying the lion's share of national and international freight. On the German road network, however, drawbar outfits still predominate, recent first-hand observation suggesting that they outnumber artics by about two to one, a statistic which happens to be difficult to reconcile with published sales figures.

For what seem to be fairly obscure reasons, the majority of truck builders have never gone into the business of supplying artic operators with more than the bare tractive units. Yet simply making the tractors is like constructing a rigid truck chassis in sawn-off form, then leaving the body builders to supply the rest of the chassis and running gear with body grafted on top. Then it is finally left to the operator to weld the two together (not literally!) to make a truck. The actual joint between the two is far from being a weld as it is the key to successful articulation. If, according to modern word usage, it seems that the resulting vehicle should be capable of fluent self-expression, the fact is that the word 'articulate' is derived from the Latin word *articulatus*, which simply means 'jointed'. In truck terms the word is accurately expressive and the main wonder of the artic lies in its possession of a standardised joint. This is known as the fifth wheel coupling and has been widely adopted throughout the world, thus allowing almost any tractive unit to be immediately coupled to any semi-trailer, which remarkable facility must amount to something of a modern miracle when considered alongside the complete lack of international, and even national, uniformity in things like railway track guages.

In the standard fifth wheel coupler, all the actual hauling strain is taken by a 2 in. diameter steel pin called the kingpin. This is set in the upper fifth wheel plate which is attached below the nose of the semi-trailer, and

A self-explanatory diagram showing the operation of the Carrymore fifth wheel coupler

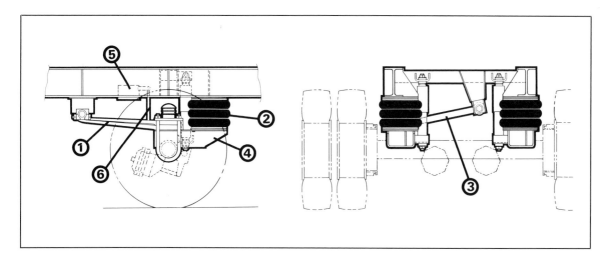

ABOVE: *The Dunlop Pneuride UT suspension system. 1 trailing link, 2 airspring, 3 Panhard rod, 4 airspring mounting, 5 chassis mounted self levelling valves and 6 valve operating levers*

ABOVE: *Custom made stepped frame. Sophisticated vans need modern advanced suspensions*

LEFT: *Low loaders seldom need detachable rear axles for the loading of tracked vehicles. They just drive on*

ABOVE LEFT: *The striped front bumper is considered an effective safety aid. TIR tilt is designed for effective customs sealing. Aerodynamic spoiler adds credibility.*

LEFT: *Tipping semi-trailers are impressive and expensive. Aluminium bodies are getting very common. Leyland's Roadtrain*

engages in jaws located in the centre of the lower fifth wheel plate which itself is carried by the rear chassis members of the tractor. Coupling up is achieved by reversing the tractor to the trailer with the two units aligned so that the kingpin can enter a vee-shaped cutout at the rear of the lower fifth wheel plate. The sides of the vee form ramps that lift the top plate on to the bottom one at the same time as the kingpin is being guided into the open jaws. With the two plates fully into position, the jaws lock automatically around the kingpin and are ready to be additionally locked manually. The complete mechanism can then serve as a turntable, which enables the tractor to carry the noseweight of the trailer, and as a hinge or pivot through which it can haul, steer and brake the load. When uncoupled, the front of the semi-trailer is supported by twin telescopic legs fitted with either small steel wheels or pads and known rather pessimistically as the 'landing gear'. After the coupling operation is completed, the legs are retracted, usually by the driver winding a folding handle. Power operation using electricity or compressed air is available but not very often fitted. Uncoupling is equally simple and quick. First, the landing gear is lowered, the manual kingpin lock released, then the tractor is driven out from under. Where a good deal of shunting of semi-trailers has to be done, a special tractive unit fitted with a hydraulically elevated fifth wheel can be employed to move semi-trailers without the landing gear having to be raised.

Clearly the semi-trailer designer is subject to the same, or similar, mandatory constraints as his counterpart working for a truck builder. Maximum overall dimensions and weights, individual axle weights, these are the main factors that have shaped the typical contemporary European vehicle. As always, a great deal of ingenuity has been exercised in the unending battle to keep unladen weights as low as possible. In the case of closed trailers, keeping the usable cubic capacity as high as possible is just as important. At one time, the general cargo carrying truck or trailer was invariably fitted with an open platform body, that is if a simple, flat platform can be truly described as a 'body'. Now more and more van type bodies are being used to give the load weather protection and to guard against pilfering. In one instance, however, even the normal wooden platform has been dispensed with. The growth of container usage has brought about the emergence of the very aptly named 'skeletal' trailer. This is no more, no less, than a bare girder-type chassis with additional cross members positioned to carry the essential twist-locks that hold the container in place. Skeletals usually come in two lengths, 20 ft and 40 ft, dimensions which are fixed by those of standard containers. Somewhat ironically, British weight limits preclude the carrying of fully loaded 40 ft 'boxes'. Current length regulations restrict semi-trailers to 40 ft (12.2 metres) overall, complete artics to 49 ft (15 metres), dimensions that naturally influence the design of virtually every tractive unit sold in Britain. Some semi-trailers are made to offer alternative kingpin positions so as to allow some flexibility in coupling to tractors with differing wheelbases. Despite this, there is no doubt that many of the tractive units imported into this country cannot be coupled to a 40 ft semi-trailer without exceeding the overall length limit. Not surprisingly, this is a sore point with home manufacturers who find that the trucks they export have to conform in every respect with the legal requirements of the country of the importer.

It was the TIR system of customs sealing that rendered the open platform truck more or less obsolete for international haulage. So the TIR tilt had to be evolved. This is a tent-like structure which fully encloses the load space of the platform, thus improving load security and facilitating sealing in accordance with the relevant customs rules. Ease of loading and unloading is always important and rigid-sided van type bodies can offer only restricted entry, usually through rear end doors although some makes do have front doors. These, of course, become accessible only after removal of the tractor. More or less the half-way stage between the tilt and the true van comes the curtain-sider, a design that provides the first class weather protection of a rigid roof whilst still allowing full length side access almost equal to that offered by the simple open platform.

What the rigid van can provide in good measure is structural strength, and in recent years more than one trailer manufacturer has harnessed this to enable him to produce chassis-less vehicles. As in modern saloon car practice, a relatively light base frame is integrated with the body to form a box structure possessing considerable strength and stiffness. Once again the target is weight saving and the consequent increasing of the payload.

Scania 112M rig for publicity in the UK. Trailer construction shows another theme again. Forty foot and more than 30 tons GVW

A good example of this type is the York Freightmaster, which is essentially a reinforced aluminium box to which the running gear is directly attached. The same maker's Fridgemaster is different only in that the box is built up from sandwich panels. In these the 'meat' is polyurethane, an excellent insulator that keeps the heat out, or the cold in, according to how you look at it, the 'bread' consisting of GRP faced plywood. Bonding these elements together produces a panel which is light, strong and a good insulator. The completed box is combined with a lightweight base frame and is again capable of being attached directly to the runner gear. The elimination of the normally 18 in. deep chassis members allows the floor to be lowered significantly, thereby increasing the cubic capacity of the van without increasing its height.

Height reduction is also the reason for the tapering of the front ends of the conventional semi-trailer chassis members to form what is known as the goose neck. Even when the load nowhere approaches the maximum permitted height (four metres in TIR operations) there is always some gain to be had in keeping it as close as possible to the ground, as lowering the centre of gravity of the vehicle is one certain way of improving its stability on the road. Increasing the possible loading height or lowering the centre of gravity can be achieved to a much greater degree by using stepped frames. These allow the main deck to be lowered and are sometimes complemented by the use of small wheels at the rear to keep

Scania 142M with windscreen visor. Trailer is stepped and tractor has second axle under the fifth wheel. Rig runs maximum length and weight

the load space unobstructed. The alternative is to accommodate the normal sized wheels in wheelboxes. For many types of work, a completely flat deck is desirable and sometimes essential to facilitate easy cargo stowage and to allow fork lift trucks to actually operate on it.

The ultimate in stepped trailers is the low loader, an apt enough description of the type in which the frame is dropped to within inches of the road level. This in itself can land the trailer in dangerous situations, as happened at a level crossing in Staffordshire when an express train hit a low loader that had grounded on the hump which is so typical of such crossings. The accident illustrated unforeseen dangers involved in the use of automatic barriers at level crossings and was instrumental in persuading the railway authorities to institute more stringent precautions. Low loaders are normally used for transporting heavy plant and machinery. The proliferation of earth moving equipment in recent years has made this type of semi-trailer much more common than it used to be. Caterpillar-tracked vehicles like bulldozers, excavators and so forth, can in effect load themselves. Smallish ones can be driven on from the side, but the big ones can only climb aboard after the trailer's rear wheels have been removed.

In contrast to the all-one-piece chunks of heavy metal the low loader is designed to carry, solids handlable as liquids such as sand, gravel, grain and so on have to be confined in high capacity bodies capable of being tipped for emptying. These are more usually fitted to rigid trucks, the heavy end of the vehicle spectrum being represented by the huge eight leggers. The tipping semi-trailer does offer a higher capacity, but is not very much favoured for work on construction sites or in sand and gravel pits where compactness and good traction ability tend to be all-important. But when off-road capability is not quite so vital the artic tipper comes into its own. In this type of combination the semi-trailer has to be supplied somehow with power for the tipping rams. This can come either from the tractor or from an auxiliary or donkey engine. Thus, the necessary hydraulic pump is driven from the tractor's power take-off incorporated in the gearbox, or directly by the donkey. One of the most impressive sights in trucking is that of a deep-sided bulk carrier all of 35 ft long elevated to a dizzy height by the telescopic rams. the maximum tipping angle is about 45 degrees and the hydraulic pressure required is as high as 1500 psi. Fine powders such as cement can be made to flow even more like liquids and are carried in trailers which look very much like liquid tankers. Engine or electrically driven pumps then do the unloading.

The trailer industry has to be just as much concerned with running gear as the truck makers, the only real difference being that semi-trailers do not have driven or steering axles. But they can have as many as three non-driven axles and it would actually be more accurate to say that sometimes they are designed to steer themselves. Wheels, tyres, brakes and suspension systems all have to perform as well as those on the tractive unit. Power for the brakes is supplied through compressed air lines from the tractor, the same supply serving as the suspension medium when the trailer is fitted with air springing. The trailer lighting circuits have also to be hooked into the tractor's system, the current being fed to the various lamps through the ubiquitous seven pin plug and socket used internationally for virtually everything from a camping trailer to a 100 ton low loader. Making mandatory the fitting of high intensity fog lamps has recently necessitated the addition of a second plug and socket.

Anyone who has travelled fairly widely in Europe will almost certainly have seen three-axled trucks running with one pair of wheels retracted clear of the road surface and a very keen observer can sometimes spot one in this country. Advocates of this system claim that it can provide substantial savings of both fuel and tyres, a very worthwhile attraction in the current economy conscious climate. In Britain its application to semi-trailers has been developed by the York Trailer Co., under the name of 'Hobo'. The York system is applied to a two axle bogie in which the front axle can be lifted by the inflation of two air bags. In fact the linkages are so arranged that the front axle is raised by $3\frac{1}{2}$ inches and the rear one lowered by the same amount. Thus the trailer can be operated with a tandem axle for maximum loading or with a single one for part-loaded or empty running. An optional extra is a load check device which enables the driver to detect overloading of the single axle. He sets the control valve to the 'check' position and if the axle is overloaded the leading axle descends and the setting is then changed to 'tandem'. As all the necessary power is drawn from the tractor's air supply, a braking circuit protection valve ensures that no air is available for Hobo operation unless the pressure in the supply line is at least 85 psi. York claim that the design of the Hobo bogey cuts out axle hop caused by severe braking on poor surfaces, while single axle running gives part- or lightweight loads a much softer ride. In view of the much more favourable spring rate it provides, the claim appears to be a very justifiable one.

Variable spring rates can be achieved with conventional multi-leaf springs simply by providing helper leaves which come into operation as the spring is deflected. But after a very long, virtually unchallenged reign the multi-leaf is tending to give way to the single or minimum (usually two) leaf spring, mainly in the interest of weight saving, a factor which has also led to the tapering of the leaves. Again, helper leaves can be used to vary the rate but a great deal of extra work has to be done by the shock absorbers to make up for the loss of damping originally provided by inter-

Dutch tanker runs fast on the German autobahn. Note trailer with three axles but only six wheels. Everything to the maximum

Conventional or normal control tractors are unusual in Europe these days. Volvo can still supply such a vehicle. This French registered rig is used for local runs only

leaf friction. Naturally, the operators most interested in variable rate suspension are those who run vehicles which cover considerable mileages when part-loaded or empty. If these happen to be simple and robust platform trailers, cushioning the empty vehicle against road shocks is not all-important except from the safety angle, as everyone must know from the way unloaded trailer wheels can dance an unpredictable jig over wavy road surfaces. On the other hand, if they happen to be specialised vehicles such as tankers, perhaps fitted with complicated valves and vulnerable pipework, they can sustain very real damage when the roads get rough. Moreover, tankers normally have to travel empty for as much as fifty per cent of every journey. They do, however, have the saving grace of carrying a load that distributes itself ideally for the maintenance of stability.

Accepting the fact that tankers and other relatively delicate vehicles need the protection of springing adaptable to varying loads, it is not entirely surprising to find that many of them are fitted with pneumatic suspension systems. As in so many engineering solutions to automotive problems, there is nothing new in the idea of suspending a road vehicle on air which is not contained inside the tyres. Pneumatic springing was being experimented with before pneumatic tyres came on the scene. In the mid 19th century suspension units were made using leather bags to confine the air. The Dunlop Pneuride system employing nylon reinforced rubber bellows to do the same job was introduced as long ago as 1958. As air at varying pressures is required to serve as the suspension medium, applying the Pneuride system to trucks adds yet another auxiliary which can be supplied with power from the normal truck braking equipment. The advantage of employing a continually renewable supply of air is in enabling the suspension units to work at continually varying pressures and thus accommodate progressively all variations of loading. Catering for these variations is the function of levelling or height control valves. These ensure that the chassis-to-road distance remains constant, therefore the vehicle can maintain its correct attitude regardless of how it is loaded. Levelling does not occur when cornering or running over rough roads, only when a 'permanent' change of attitude takes place. The weak points about such a system in its simplest form include a rather feeble resistance to steering-induced roll, a complete lack of self-damping ability such as the multi-leaf spring exhibits, and little capacity to prevent lateral displacement of the axle. All these defects are more or less curable and Dunlop use rubber springs coupled to trailing links to provide roll stiffness, hydraulic shock absorbers to do the necessary damping, and a transverse beam known as a panhard rod to securely locate the axle. As with all ancillaries taking air from the brake supply, priority is given to the latter by a valve which refuses to feed the suspension units (or their reservoir) until the line pressure has risen to 65 psi. Dunlop air springs form the basis of other suspension systems such as the York Harcopoise. Here, though, they are employed in combination with multi-leaf springs. There is no added mechanical roll stiffness as in the Pneuride, but a panhard rod and telescopic hydraulic dampers do the same duty as in the Dunlop set-up.

York, Crane Fruehauf and Trailor are the big names in trailer manufacture and all have plants in Britain and overseas. Vehicles designed to carry liquid cargoes, however, belong to the domain of specialists like Thompson, builders of road tankers for more than 50 years. These are designed to transport the whole range of liquids . . . milk and other foods (including beer), petroleum products, chemicals and other miscellaneous fluids. The various types of liquid pose their own problems for the tank maker but the production of suitable running gear is left to the trailer makers. Foods demand a high standard of hygiene and the design and construction of suitable tanks has to provide for easy cleaning. The materials normally used are high quality stainless steel and aluminium, insulation, where required, being by polystyrene or glass fibre. Tank capacities go up to just under 5000 gallons, a weight of just about 22 tons if the fluid is mainly water. With this aboard, tractor and trailer unladen weights have to be kept well down to avoid exceeding the British limit of 32 tons. Temperature control of foods is clearly important so heating and lagging can be incorporated. The maximum volume of petroleum products to be carried in one tanker is restricted by law to 6600 gallons and here again artic designers have their work cut out to accommodate this without going over the gross weight limit. Anything from innocuous distilled water to highly poisonous and/or corrosive fluids goes into chemical tankers which are normally made from mild steel, the same material with a lining, or stainless steel. Effluent tankers are in much the same league and subject to the same stringent safety regulations. Thompson add massive side rails where protection against tank rupture in side-swipe or roll-over accidents is required. Container carriers can also become tankers, as the addition of end or full length frames converts a simple tank into a standard container capable of being carried by skeletals and platforms equipped with the necessary twist-locks. If the tank is totally enclosed, it looks like any other container and there is less chance of the contents being tapped illegally.

7 Geared for speed

*Top gear trucks . . . not so simple . . . obedient cogs . . . judging the revs . . .
constant mesh gaining . . . arrival of the double H . . . enormous versatility
. . . semi-automatic . . . fully auto . . . fuel efficiency peak . . . axles and
weights . . . effective checks needed.*

Long distance trucks spend around seventy per cent of their running time
in top gear, so one of the leading makers of truck transmissions has
claimed. The statistic was quoted to support the premise that the
simplest of transmissions is the most efficient one. This is because every
extra element in the drive train absorbs at least some energy. No-one can
justifiably quarrel with this argument, yet in any survey of heavy trucks
designed for long haul use it is very difficult to find models offered with
transmissions which seem to merit being described as 'simple'. So,
although it is probably true to say that for nearly three quarters of his
time at the wheel the long distance trucker can more or less ignore the
gear lever, it is also true to say that for the remainder of any particular
stint he is likely to be having to stir gears aplenty; perhaps only nine,
maybe as many as thirteen, or possibly even sixteen of them! This simply
has to be a bewildering array of ratios for the outsider, or even for the
experienced motorist who prides himself on his neat handling of a five
speed gearbox.

The study of truck transmissions generates even more bewilderment
when it comes to be appreciated that the basic commercial vehicle
gearbox likewise provides no more than four or five ratios. The puzzle is
resolved only when it is understood that the multiplication of the ratios
depends on supplementary devices which usually have their own
selection arrangement. So the trucker very often has much more than the
conventional gear lever to play with. The extra controls may be designed
to operate a 'splitter', a 'range-changer' or, more rarely, a two speed axle.
Each one of these mechanisms can double the number of available gear
ratios, and when, as is frequently the case, two of them are included in the
drive line, as many as sixteen gears can be at the finger tips of the driver
who knows how to use them.

For reasons both obvious and obscure, truck gearbox design has
refused to become standardized in the way it has for those supplied to the
private motorist. The manual box that car drivers know so well invariably
offers the luxury of easy gear engagement under all conditions. For this
they have to thank the synchromesh mechanism which, as its name
implies, synchronizes the speeds of the gears before engagement. But
things are very different for the European trucker who might spend one

ABOVE RIGHT: *Eaton Fuller 7200
series twin countershaft gearbox
with 13 speeds*

ABOVE FAR RIGHT: *Eaton's 25100
axle is a single reduction type, and
is fitted with 'S' cam brakes*

RIGHT: *The Spicer SST10 10
speed splitter gearbox as fitted to
the Leyland 16.28 Roadtrains*

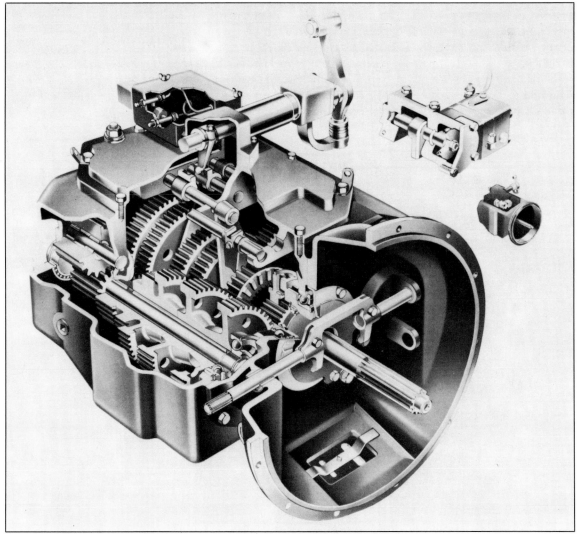

day relying on the dog clutches synchronising themselves into engagement, only to find that a change of trucks next morning requires him to synchronize the gear speeds himself by putting in a lot of nimble work with his feet. When this actually happens, it is odds on that the second vehicle is equipped with an American designed gearbox. Rather paradoxically, the land where the gear stick once became virtually extinct as far as the car driver was concerned, has always expected its truckers to acquire the technique of double declutching. This involves speeding up the engine in mid-change with the clutch engaged and the gear lever in neutral. Accurate judgement of the revs needed to bring the relevant dogs to the same speeds then allows the gear lever to be pushed home easily and without any sign of a crunch, the onlooker getting no hint that the gearbox is of the type known as 'constant mesh', and once dubbed the 'crash' type because of the noises many drivers extracted from it. There can be no doubt that the constant mesh box is the more robust and durable of the two types, rewarding real skill with faster changes requiring less effort at the lever. Slowing down the dog clutches in a synchromesh box does require a heftier push on the stick and lever breakages have been known to occur. It would be logical to assume that the majority of drivers prefer the more positive if slower changing of the synchro box, but this seems to be far from the truth. Many of them believe that the possession of the skill necessary to achieve quiet constant mesh changes sets the truly professional driver apart from the ruck of

The ZF WSK400 converter and clutch unit with the six speed synchromesh S6-90 gearbox. In layman's terms a Transmatic semi-automatic truck gearbox

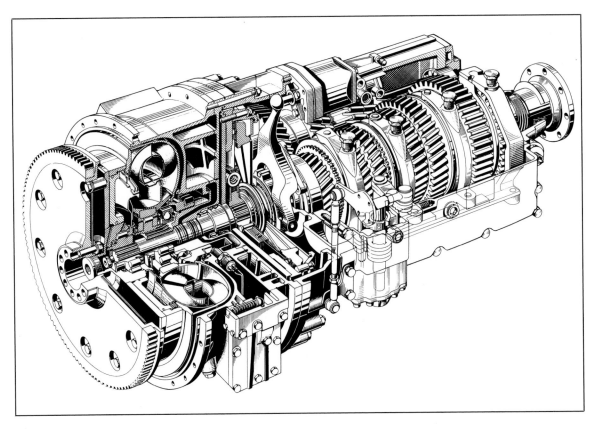

amateurs; there is no way in which a run-of-the-mill car driver is going to be able to drive his truck satisfactorily, even if the law allowed him to try. However, a cynic might ask: 'who needs synchromesh when most of the running time is spent firmly in top gear?' He might also point out that there must be some relevance in the fact that American inter-city road conditions make for few demands on the gearbox, and the far reaching spread of motorways across Europe has brought running conditions very much closer to those existing in the USA.

Whatever the reason, the fact is that constant mesh in Europe is gaining ground at the expense of synchromesh; very much to the fore in this trend are the various models of Eaton Fuller gearboxes. The first products of the Eaton Corporation of Cleveland, Ohio, were truck axles. Then in 1958 a take-over of Fuller Manufacturing set the corporation on the road to becoming America's leading producer of truck transmissions. Since 1965 Eaton Fuller gearboxes have been manufactured in Britain, first in Manchester, then at an additional plant in Basingstoke. Widely fitted by both British and continental truck builders, the Eaton Fuller range-change boxes are designed to provide nine or 13 speeds and equipped with twin countershafts to divide the torque stresses and keep down casing lengths and weights. The availability of two ratio ranges is made possible by the fitting of an extra unit on the output shaft which serves as a two speed gearbox—synchromesh this time! The top gear of the two speeder converts the output of the main gearbox to the high

Scania's range of self-built power train components. Two engines are straight sixes, the other a massive V8. Note the size of the brake drums on the rear axles

range, the bottom gear converts it to the low range. A pneumatic or electrical switch sited on or near the gear lever operates the range-changer. A recently introduced option offers range selection directly by the gear lever. The latter has a shift pattern in the form of a double 'H', the change from one range to another being accomplished by the gear stick tripping a switch as it is moved across the bridge linking the two gates. With the basic gearbox plus range-change providing nine speeds to choose from, the ratios are widely spread to cater for the most extreme conditions—from crawling up the steepest gradients to running at maximum speed along a motorway. The Fuller's step up to a thirteen speeder is achieved by adding a splitter unit to the input end of the basic gearbox' which enables the driver to select in-between ratios that effectively double the number of available speeds, but does nothing to increase the overall gap between top and bottom gears.

Adding both splitter and range-changer to the basic gearbox is obviously a recipe for enormous versatility, but current indications are that engine developments may reduce the need to employ them all together. With the emphasis now being placed on obtaining wider torque spreads from lower revving diesels, ultra close ratios are tending to become less of a necessity, more an under-used luxury. Then the choice can become an either/or one by fitting a splitter to a wide ratio main gearbox. This point has recently been demonstrated by Leyland in choosing to equip the first Roadtrains with a US designed Spicer five speed constant mesh box with splitter. The superseded Marathon II was given a similar spread of ratios by fitting an Eaton Fuller range-change nine speeder, the Spicer, of course, providing 10 speeds.

The Scandinavian truck-making twins (far from identical ones), Scania and Volvo, remain completely committed to synchromesh. Typically Scania is a 10 speed splitter type box while Volvo includes both a splitter and range-changer to pack 16 ratios into a box with wide driver-appeal. Until recently, Daimler Benz, the German truck-making giant, was also completely committed to fitting synchro boxes to its Mercedes models, but these are now available equipped with constant mesh Eaton Fullers. Previously to this sharp change in direction, Daimler Benz had either built its own gearboxes or bought them from another German company, ZF (Zahnradfabrik Friedrichshafen). Very much the transmission specialists, ZF are able to supply virtually any and every gearbox variation . . . constant mesh, synchromesh, both with and without splitter and range-change units, semi-automatic and fully automatic. Named the Transmatic, the ZF semi-auto transmission was specifically designed for use in heavy trucks. In the Transmatic, the normal clutch is replaced by a torque converter through which the engine drives a conventional synchromesh gearbox. A shift clutch is interposed between converter and gearbox and this has to be released for gear selection in the normal way, but then the converter takes over to provide a clutchless getaway. Once the truck is well on the move, the converter locks up to provide a solid drive between engine and gearbox. As speed falls or the driver kicks down the accelerator, the converter unlocks and, in the latter case, begins to multiply the torque to allow him to stave off a

No one can deny that many roads are not fit for the job. Looked at another way, the heavy trucks are too big. Two fifty footers meet at a tight village turn in Northern France. DAF going away, Pegaso coming

down change or changes. ZF claim that under busy urban conditions a thinking driver can virtually eliminate gear shifting, running entirely on the torque converter and thus relieved of much of the stress and danger involved in threading a big truck through dense traffic. If intelligent operation is the key to getting the best out of the Transmatic system, this should be a point very much in its favour for the trucker who takes pride in his skills.

The ZF fully automatic transmission is conventional in design and has a strong competitor in the one built for truck use by the Allison Division of the mighty General Motors. Both ZF and Allison automatics have been specified by some British operators and at least one has claimed that leaving gear changing entirely to the gearbox can actually improve fuel consumption, but this must be true only of certain types of running, and these obviously cannot include long hauls over fast roads. Torque converters do, however, cushion the drive line, and thus give associated components a much easy time than when the drive is taken through a friction clutch, even if the latter is controlled by a skilled driver.

Whatever the type of gearbox employed, at the other end of the drive line there will usually be a spiral bevel or hypoid live rear axle with its drive shafts either directly connected to the wheel hubs or turning them through planetary reduction gears. Dividing into two the task of bringing propeller shaft speed down to road wheel speed, as in the second case, is a means of easing the torque load on the drive shafts at the expense of some extra friction. In addition, the differential casing of a double reduction axle can be made smaller and thus has more ground clearance. A two speed axle acts as a supplementary gearbox in much the same way as a range-changer, doubling the number of available ratios. Air pressure is usually the power made to change the axle's gears, and it normally operates the differential lock fitted to many final drives as a means of improving traction on slippery surfaces.

But to get back to the long haul truck which allegedly spends so much of its running time in top gear, it does seem likely that in the not too distant future an adequate road performance and better economy will be obtainable from a gearbox containing relatively few gears and driving through a single reduction axle. This is assuming that engine development stays on its present course with torque spreads widening and crankshaft speeds falling. Low engine speeds demand the use of high (numerically low) axle ratios and telling comparisons can be made between the gearing of trucks and that of private cars. The ordinary car is seldom geared to achieve a road speed as high as 20 mph with the engine turning over at 1000 rpm in top gear. On the other hand, top weight trucks are often geared to achieve as much as 30 to 35 mph at 1000 rpm in top. However, judging by the varying trends of the past, there is no way of knowing if the low revving, slow burning diesel is here to stay. The chances are that it is, but clearly if continuing research into the complex combustion processes yields data which persuades designers to bring back higher engine speeds, then transmissions will have to be modified to make best use of them. For the moment, the long-legged truck cruising at around 65 mph with its crankshaft revolving at a mere 1800 rpm represents the peak of fuel efficiency. Low engine speeds are also beneficial in reducing both mechanical noise and wear rates. The same could be said of road speeds if the journey time element did not come in to confuse the picture.

Wheels rather than axles govern the system used for classifying trucks. Thus a two-axled tractive unit is known as 4 × 2, the first figure being the total number of wheels, the second the number of driven wheels.

Built for South Africa this ERF 'Fuel Saver' model 60 B series 6 × 4 tractor incorporates many European specifications. The cab is EEC crash approved and can tilt through 68 degrees. Will the UK allow its use?

LEFT: *Spanish Pegaso 352CV (horsepower) is as modern as any other European truck. Semi shows length – disadvantageous in tight corners*

RIGHT: *6 × 4 Ford Transcontinental illustrates British ideas on the draw bar trailer outfit. Some pundits maintain that this method of hauling is better than the traditional articulated one*

BELOW: *4 × 2 Scania rig shows three not two axles on the trailer. Compare this with the Ford directly above*

Somewhat confusingly, double wheels are counted as singles. A double drive tractor has 4 driven wheels, hence is known as a 6 × 4, similarly a rigid eight legger with double drive comes out as an 8 × 4, Semi-trailers, though, are treated completely differently, being classified as single-axled, twin or tandem axled, or tri-axled.

Axles are also important in what is known as the plating system which was introduced in the 1967 Road Traffic Act. Then every goods vehicle weighing more than 30 cwt unladen had to be tested and marked with maximum permitted weights. At long last the irrelevance of unladen weights in the context of the law was acknowledged. Since then maximum permitted gross weights and individual axle weights have been the subjects of great debates, on the one hand the transport industry claiming that heavier vehicles can be operated more efficiently, on the other the environmentalists asserting that increasing maximum weights would bring more noise, pollution, danger and damage to buildings and roads.

Various attempts have been made to assess the amount of road damage caused by heavy vehicles. This is clearly no easy task and any figures produced are immediately seized upon by people with axes to grind and made to mean what they want them to mean. The fairly widespread breaking up of British motorways has naturally been blamed on the heavy truck but no one seems to have stopped to consider what state the motorways would be in if they had never been used at all during their twenty years of existence. Anyone who has seen the results of the unchecked attacks of nature on every sort of paving knows that these can be more damaging than the constant pounding of heavily loaded wheels. This being so, estimates of the so-called track costs of the bigger trucks must be looked on with a very great deal of suspicion.

The most recent and best reasoned shots in the battle of the weights were fired by the Armitage Committee in a report which asserted that the most effective recipe for minimising road damage was strict limitation of individual axle loadings. There is no sign yet that this significant premise has been accepted by the government, but presumably one day some increase in maximum gross weights will be permitted as long as the number of axles is multiplied accordingly. Then, as mentioned elsewhere in this book, five and six axled artics are likely to become as commonplace as four axled ones are now. It does seem, however, that one of the prerequisites for the implementation of the Armitage proposals should be the establishment of an effective weight checking system along all the busy trucking routes. Weigh stations are very much a feature of the US Interstate Highway network and will have to become as big a part of the British road scene. That way some of the sharpest teeth of the anti-truck lobby could be drawn and responsible operators would to a great extent be freed from the unfair competition of hauliers prepared to take the risk of running overloaded vehicles. Weight checks at the ports have yielded ample evidence showing that continental trucks coming in are sometimes over-weight. This must be pretty galling for the law abiding British operator, particularly when he sees that many of them are overlength as well.

8 Braked for safety

Naked horsepower . . . confusion of the brakes . . . devised by Westinghouse
. . . there for the taking . . . instant muscle . . . separate circuits . . . first regs
. . . spring actuators . . . disc trial . . . dreaded jack-knife . . . changing
braking equation . . . total loss . . . acknowledged crudity.

Big trucks need big engines and as the latter have grown in size and power output so has the glamour that naturally attaches to so much naked horse power. In days gone by, rear-mounted signs warning that the truck in front had brakes of some particular type or make were presumably intended to inform following drivers that it could stop as well as go. The unpalatable truth is that, even in the days when power outputs were puny, trucks could go better than they could stop, and with current power outputs it is always easier to impress by quoting how well a truck goes rather than how well it stops. Ideally, the braking performance of heavy commercial vehicles should match the standard set by the best passenger cars; the fact that it does not makes the motorways much less safe than they should be.

In Europe, at least, the disc brake revolution fizzled out before it really hit the truck scene, but there is no reason to suggest that the wide-spread adoption of discs in place of drums would have changed the situation very dramatically. Anyone who has inspected the sectioned chassis at a commercial motor show will have seen the massive drums and linings normally used and will have appreciated that lack of stopping power at the wheels is not a problem. The main problem in trying to stop a big truck quickly and safely lies in the wide range of circumstances encountered between the empty and the loaded states. Thus a trucker outward bound with a full load could be trying to keep in check as much as 32 tons, and on his way home sitting in the same cab controlling the same braking system he might be holding back no more than a mere 12 tons. Not only has the total weight changed dramatically, it has also been redistributed, and not only to the confusion of the brakes, the suspension has every right to be just as put out. Some of the worst effects of this transformation can be avoided by the adoption of variable rate suspension and the fitting of load apportioning valves to gear braking effort to axle weight. These are, however, mere palliatives and there can be no denying the fact that the universal fitment of some type of anti-lock braking is long overdue. But more of this later.

The type of basic braking system fitted to most of the world's heavy trucks was originally devised by George Westinghouse as long ago as 1869. In this compressed air is used both as a means of applying engine power to braking and of transmitting it from brake pedal to each wheel. One of the main advantages of using air is simply that it is there for the taking, and can safely be bled back into the atmosphere from whence it came. Though it may seem as if relying on a gas, which is clearly difficult to confine under pressure in any system of pipes and chambers, would make for unreliability, air operation has been made completely reliable without resorting to undue complication or sophistication in the equipment required. It offers designers a great deal of flexibility both when laying out brake installations and when fitting in the various auxiliaries that have come to be either air assisted or air powered. Air as a suspension medium offers an elegant means of providing variable rate springing, as a form of instant muscle for the driver it can help apply the parking brake, assist with gear changing and operating the clutch, and even lighten the effort needed to turn the steering wheel, although this task is more often given over to hydraulic pressure, as it is in many of the bigger cars.

The source of the compressed air is normally a twin cylinder engine driven compressor which runs continuously to charge reservoirs that store the accumulated energy for release when needed. As soon as the required working pressure is reached, an unloader valve operates automatically to allow the compressor to run light until more air has to be pumped into the reservoirs to maintain the pressure. A dashboard indicator warns the driver of any undue loss of pressure. When he treads on the brake pedal it simply opens a valve which allows air to flow to brake chambers containing pressure sensitive diaphragms and mounted close to or directly on the brake back-plates. Under pressure the chamber diaphragms move and through a mechanical or hydraulic linkage apply the brake shoes to the drums. In actual practice, the full flow of air does not always pass through the brake pedal valve, the flow through the latter often being used to operate relay valves that connect the brake chambers directly to the reservoirs, thus promoting a freer flow though at the same time reducing the amount of air required. Again, a single foot valve is not used, dual valves are fitted so that depressing the pedal causes air to be fed simultaneously to two completely separate circuits and thus minimises the risk of total circuit failure. Simple check valves ensure that air does not flow from a sound to a failed circuit. In damp climates, atmospheric air often contains a great deal of moisture, some of which invariably condenses in the reservoirs. Therefore these have to be fitted with drain valves, primarily as a defence against the water freezing and blocking pipes or seizing moving parts. The drain valves may be manually or automatically opened. Alcohol evaporators form another line of defence against the freezing danger. The spirit is introduced into the system via the compressor and then serves as an anti-freeze agent. Perhaps the best defence against atmospheric moisture is the incorporation of an air dryer to ensure that only dry air is supplied to the pressure reservoirs.

It may seem hard to believe that the first British regulations specifically concerned with truck braking performance were not brought into force until 1964. The performance requirements then set meant that trucks had to match those set for passenger cars, 0.5 g for the service brakes,

ABOVE: *Seddon Atkinson and Girling cooperated to produce this experimental disc brake system*

BELOW: *Girling's more conventional Mk II Twinstop*

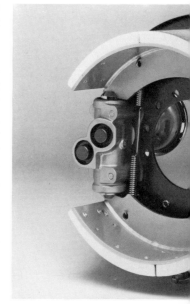

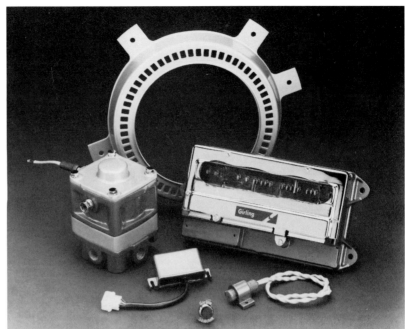

ABOVE RIGHT: *The components of the Skidchek system from Girling*

RIGHT: *Inside the Dunlop Maxaret anti-skid system*

0.25 g for an independent secondary system. Nothing specific was said about the performance expected from the parking brake. Then in 1968 additional regulations specified that the parking brake had to be capable of holding the vehicle securely on a 1 in 6 gradient. At this time agreement was reached between the Ministry of Transport and the industry on a Code of Practice recommending that design standards should aim to better the legal requirements. The result was that designers began to set their sights on service and secondary performances of 0.6 g and a park brake hold on a 1 in 5. One previous requirement, the necessity for the parking brake to be applied and held mechanically was modified to specify that it had only to be held mechanically.

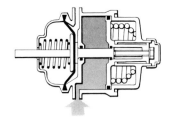

Bendix spring brake chamber. Normal driving

A quite significant change, this, as it made possible the air operation of the parking brake. Strictly speaking, it would be more correct to say that air pressure could be used to release the parking brake. The fail safe system adopted employed powerful springs to force the shoes into contact with the drums. The springs are contained inside a chamber similar to the diaphragm chambers of the service and secondary systems, the whole mechanism being known as a spring brake actuator. In practice, the spring brake chamber is usually combined with the diaphragm chamber used for the service brake. During normal running, the park brake control valve supplies air at a constant pressure to the spring brake piston, thereby compressing the spring and holding off the brakes. In this condition the service brake is applied in the normal way by the opening of the footbrake valve. Moving the hand valve lever away from the 'off' position gradually releases air pressure from the spring brake chamber and spring pressure then provides progressive secondary braking to back up the service brake. On parking, the hand control valve is used to exhaust air completely from the spring brake chambers, thus applying the brake under the full tension of the spring. The vehicle cannot then be moved until sufficient air pressure is available to hold off the brake spring, or a manual release bolt is turned to wind off the tension.

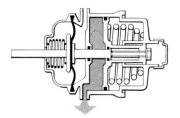

Secondary and parking brake

The disc brake has so far failed to make much headway on trucks because of the difficulty of dissipating the vast amounts of heat generated in stopping the heaviest vehicles. Discs can normally be allowed to run hotter than drums without losing stopping power due to fade, but drums have won up to now because they can be increased in width when further increases in diameter are not possible. The disc can only be expanded in diameter and wheel size is clearly the limiting factor. One way of accelerating the possible heat loss is to increase the maximum possible operating temperature and the key to this lies in the development of new friction materials; another way is to use multiple discs. There is no doubt that modern trucks need disc brakes and are certain to get them in time. They need the smooth, progressive retardation that discs can provide as there is safety in smoothness, especially when the road surface is slippery. The National Freight Corporation is currently sponsoring the evaluation of a disc system fitted to the front wheels of a Seddon Atkinson 32 ton tractor and its seems unlikely this is the only trial in progess.

Predictably, however, the system which has been credited with

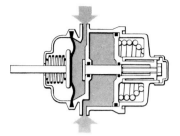

Service brake

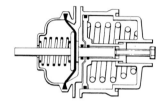

Manual release

endowing the new Leyland T45 with a braking performance that sets new standards is one that still employs drums. Known as the Girling Twinstop, it provides two leading shoe efficiency with automatic lining adjustment and thus requires the minimum of servicing. The drums are 15.5 in. in diameter, 7.87 in. wide, and house shoes carrying linings which are $\frac{3}{4}$ in. thick. These shoes are expanded by wedges that do a job more often done on trucks by 'S' shaped cams. The latter require mechanical linkages to translate the fore and aft movement of the air operated diaphragms into a rotary one. In the Twinstop, the brake chambers can be mounted on the brake backplate with the diaphragms coupled directly to the wedge expanders. Dual operating circuits are provided by linking each actuator to the corresponding ones at the other wheels, so that in the event of circuit failure all-wheel braking at 60 per cent of the normal service brake performance is still available. Spring actuators can be fitted all round if two leading shoe parking power is required.

The 1968 Code of Practice agreed between the industry and the MOT had something to say on the desirability of the brakes not impairing stability, in particular they were not to cause jack-knifing. A somewhat pious hope, this, as any system capable of locking the rear wheels of an artic tractor can undoubtedly cause jack-knifing. The term is a fairly self-explanatory one describing the involuntary pivoting of tractor and trailer about the combination's kingpin that folds them together just as a blade folds into the handle of a jack-knife. At best it does no more than damage the tractor's cab, at worst it spells injury or death for the driver and maybe for other road users unfortunate enough to be within range of the rampaging truck.

The one certain preventative of this behaviour is some means of keeping the tyres firmly gripping the road at all times, so that the wheels never lock. In fact, anti-lock braking systems have been in existence for very many years. One of the best known is that offered by Dunlop under the name of Maxaret. This was originally developed for aircraft use and over the succeeding years was made available to the private motorist on models that unfortunately failed to survive. The fate of this very necessary technological advance has been not quite so depressing in the truck world, as some safety conscious heavy transport operators have had Maxaret fitted to their artic tractors for more than a decade. Girling, already mentioned as manufacturers of the Twinstop braking system, are also into anti-lock with the Skidchek device designed to keep the wheels turning at all times. The principles of operation of the two systems are very similar. A slotted metal disc revolves with the wheel and its behaviour is monitored electronically. The imminence of wheel locking can be sensed and a signal to release the brake is sent to the control valve. Maxaret also employs propeller shaft sensing to monitor the behaviour of the drive axle of the tractor. Of just as much importance as the avoidance of the dreaded jack-knife is preventing any of the wheels of an artic from losing their grip on the road. If the wheels of the semi-trailer lock, a potentially lethal side-stepping known as trailer swing can result. If the same thing happens to the front wheels of the tractor the driver can be faced with a complete loss of steering control. This was seen to happen to a somewhat recklessly driven Mercedes artic somewhere in France. Instead of taking a long easy bend through a village, the truck mounted the kerb and swept through the massed tables of a large, pavement cafe, fortunately, without killing anyone as the rain that had made the road greasy had also kept the customers inside. So simple jack-knife elimination is not enough, it should be made a near impossibility for a top weight truck to run amok in this way.

The Hope Anti Jack-knife Device: Top *the Hope kingpin,* with below *the standard, conventional pin built to SAE specification*

From now on it should happen less and less to this German maker's trucks as Mercedes too, have become involved in the successful development of an anti-lock braking system. Wabco, the German subsidiary of the American Automotive Products Group, has partnered the truck side of Daimler Benz during the development of the ABS system, one which was first applied to high performance cars. Basically, ABS is similar in principle to the other electronic skid control systems although Mercedes do claim that it achieves greater delicacy of detection and correction of incipient wheel-locking, and have carried out some convincing demonstrations on ice to prove this. A problem likely to be encountered by operators of artics using any of these anti-lock devices is the changing braking equation presented to a driver who may have all the wheels of his tractor/trailer combination protected from locking on one trip; then next time out with a different tractor and trailer, perhaps only the drive wheels of the tractor have protection; then the next time on the road with his original unit all the wheels of the tractor and again none of the trailer's. The least that can be done now is to make the various types of anti-lock system compatible with one another. One step in the right direction has been made as part of a project undertaken by the Motor Industry Research Association and financed by the Department of Industry. The aim of the project is the development of an SAV or Safety Articulated Vehicle, and a start was made by equipping a Leyland Roadtrain tractor with the Girling Skidchek anti-lock system, actually a factory-fitted option on the Roadtrain. The tractor was then hitched to a semi-trailer equipped with Dunlop's Maxaret skid control gear and the two systems successfully operated together.

But not everyone agrees that the only way to prevent jack-knifing is to fit anti-lock brakes. The Hope anti jack-knife device is designed to be fitted to the trailer, not the tractor. It operates at the kingpin to control any rotational forces which happen to be present before they have chance to build up to danger level. Motorists who tow two wheeled trailers will recognize a similarity between the Hope device and the so-called stabilisers designed to damp out unwanted energy at the coupling. The main difference is that the former is wholly controlled through the braking system. It is basically an air-operated multi-disc slipping clutch coupled to the kingpin, and is brought into operation every time the brakes are applied. Then the discs are squeezed together and offer resistance to kingpin rotation in proportion to and slightly ahead of the braking effort at the wheels. It is argued that any initial move out of alignment has to be killed quickly if the build up of dangerous forces is to be avoided. The damping effort has no effect on normal articulation.

RIGHT: *The basic components of the Hope Anti Jack-knife Device. The kingpin is right at the bottom. This is geared to a series of friction plates, a piston and cylinder head. Numbering scheme comes from parts list*

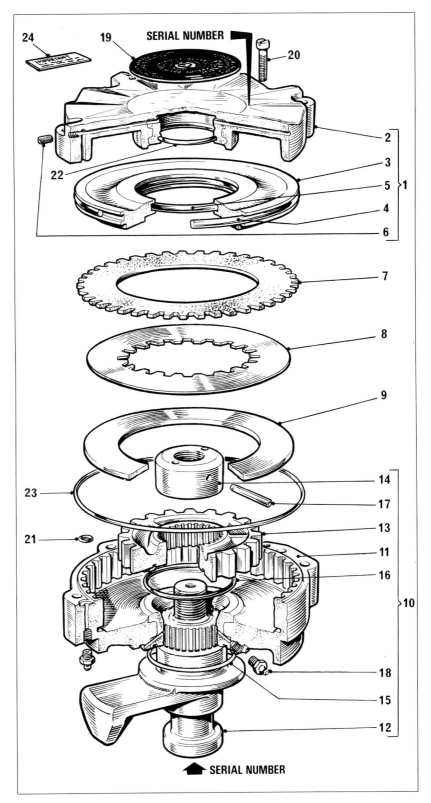

Stopping a truck in an emergency is one thing, controlling its speed on long down gradients is quite another. Descents that can be many miles long in mountainous country demand the absorption of an enormous amount of energy if a rolling truck is not to be speeded out of control. The energy absorbed has inevitably to be dissipated in the form of heat and in conventional drum brakes the rate of dissipation has to be high enough to prevent temperatures rising to the level where brake fade can arise. Severe fade can bring about a total loss of stopping power and the possible consequences can then be truly horrific. As any motorist knows, using the engine to slow a car on long down grades takes some of the strain off the brakes. Truck drivers naturally do this even more so and usually have an added card up their sleeves in the form of an exhaust brake. This, in effect, throttles the exhaust system and thereby increases the braking effort the engine can muster. Again, the key factor is heat dissipation and this then occurs via the normal engine cooling system which clearly has a great deal of reserve capacity during downhill running. A more effective way of increasing the retarding ability of the power unit is to modify the operation of the valves, and this is done in an American device known as the Jakebrake. Also originating in America, the Caterpillar Brakesaver is a hydraulic retarder built into the engine flywheel. It resembles a torque converter working in reverse and uses the same oil as the engine.

Yet another way of absorbing surplus energy is to turn it into electricity which, in turn, can be dissipated as heat. If electric vehicles ever take over the trucking scene, then the driving motors will certainly be designed to serve as generators during downhill running. This is common practice on electric railways, particularly on mountain sections where the rail cars used carry great banks of resistors on their roofs. Current generated by the traction motors serving as retarders is fed through the resistors which turn it into heat and the cold mountain air does the rest. Electrical methods tend to make for more elegant solutions to problems concerning energy control than mechanical ones, and as applied to trucks the electrical or magnetic retarder does get away from the acknowledged crudity of rubbing a friction lining on the inside of a metal drum. The Telma electro-magnetic retarder hails from France and employs the vehicle propeller shaft to turn a rotor set between the poles of a stator mounted on the chassis. The stator carries electro-magnets which are energised by the vehicle battery. Four independent circuits can be switched in progressively to provide a steady increase in braking torque. Heat dissipation is claimed to be rapid enough to allow the retarder to be used continuously for unlimited periods of time. The consequent increase in the life expectancy of the drums and linings of the service braking system is said to be of the order of five to 10 times.

9 Diesel technology

*Safety or political . . . lead or feathers . . . new Ford . . . running for cover . . .
torquey Gardner . . . prolific Perkins . . . Eagle story . . . neck and neck
Cummins . . . cooling the charge . . . survivor ERF . . . Foden Inc . . . IH means
SA . . . lonely Leyland . . . two stroke Bedford . . . Volvo rejects . . . Scania
rejects . . . in-house Daf's . . . modular Mercs . . . dry Maggies . . . massive
Fiat . . . rotary Renaults . . . wide-spec. Mans.*

The mechanical development of the long haul truck has always been
subject to ever-changing influences. Fuel availability and price have had
the most impact in recent years, though it would be wrong to overlook the
massive effects of legislation whether enacted in the name of safety,
protection of the environment, or for various political reasons. Although
the transporting of goods by road has always had a clear economic lead
over all other ways of moving freight over land, neither truck operators
nor truck builders can ever afford to lose sight of the fact that the prime
function of any goods vehicle is to make profits for them both. But first, of
course, they have to take a long hard look at the laws of the land where the
vehicle in question will spend most of its operating life. Maximum
permissible gross weights, maximum axle weights, maximum overall
dimensions, minimum power to weight ratios, any noise and emission
restrictions—these are the sort of things that determine design
parameters and thus put the designer in a strait jacket before ever he can
plot a single line on his drawing board.

Working within these externally determined constraints he has to
make sure that the truck which finally drives off the end of the production
line is one able to compete successfully in terms of payload, running costs
and, naturally, first cost. His task is complicated further by the need to
take account of the different types of load his new model is likely to be
hauling. The old tag about which is the heavier, a pound of lead or a
pound of feathers, is a reminder that there are more things to consider in
truck design than sheer weight of cargo. So with many types of
merchandise the provision of the maximum possible cubic capacity is of
more importance; a truck just big enough to carry twenty tons of lead
would be hard put to accommodate a single ton of feathers. The task of
providing for both is, of course, simplified in the case of the tractive unit
as it can be hitched to any suitable semi-trailer. Where volume is of prime
concern, however, the separate trailer has a lot to offer, so the draw-bar
outfit is far from dead and is indeed more in evidence on the German
autobahn network than the artic.

Once upon a time (and this must sound like a fairy tale to the present
generation of designers and development engineers) it was possible to
design and produce a totally new vehicle and actually be able to pay for

the development costs out of revenue. With such costs now rivalling the revenues of countries rather than companies the most that can be achieved can only be described as piecemeal re-designing and development. Thus, an allegedly new truck might be merely a new cab clothing old mechanicals. With the cab development costs hopefully paid off, a new or extensively revised engine design might be considered. Then will come the turn of the transmission and so on.

There is, however, another side to the picture, one made possible by the considerable growth of the major components industry. Apparently in total contradiction of the statements made in the previous paragraph, the Ford Motor Company in 1975 launched a completely new range of premium long distance trucks. 'The concept', Ford claimed, 'was to assemble in one vehicle the best available components in the business, components which had proved their toughness and reliability in world-wide operation'. Judging by the specification of the Transcontinental, as the new truck was called, the recipe according to Ford for the successful making of a premium truck consisted of a Cummins turbocharged six cylinder in-line diesel engine (with choice of four power ratings from 240 to 345 bhp) driving through a Spicer air/hydraulic self-adjusting twin plate clutch and an Eaton Fuller constant mesh 9 or 13 speed gearbox to a Rockwell single reduction axle. The Transcontinental was, in effect, an up-to-the-minute design made possible by the sharing of the development costs with the other users of the proprietary components judged by Ford to be the 'best in the business'.

For reasons that are far from being immediately obvious, Ford's bold sally into the competitive world of European top weight trucks has proved less successful than it might have been. Built in Amsterdam for the first hald dozen years of its existence, the Transconti, as it came to be known, is now assembled at Langley in Buckinghamshire alongside the highly successful ranges of Ford medium weight trucks. When the ever-rising price of diesel fuel had operators running for cover in the shape of more economical engines, Ford had simply to drop in the Cummins E series units to update the Transconti, all the necessary development having been done by the engine builders and paid for by their customers.

The marrying of major components from specialist sources is nothing new in Britain and it is very much the way things are done on the other side of the Atlantic. In Britain the diesel revolution brought a specialist engine builder, the Manchester firm of L. Gardner & Sons, to the forefront. Now part of the Hawker Siddeley conglomerate, Gardner are still very much in the business of building automotive diesels which have earned an enviable reputation for reliability and low maintenance costs. Staying faithful to the in-line cylinder arrangement, the six and eight cylinder Gardners are naturally aspirated units of 10.5 and 14 litres capacity respectively, and are noted for their torquey, economical performance which owes a lot to the fact that Gardner kept peak engine revs down when all around were increasing theirs. Now most of the others have come back into line with Gardner. With 265 bhp now available from the eight cylinder version, this is an option likely to be widely chosen by operators in the top weight bracket. Also, at long last Gardner

The modern truck looks much like this. The changes we can look forward to in the future will need to be radical to change outwardly this familiar picture. Advancing technology will conserve fuel by reducing weight, streamlining bodywork and increasing engine efficiency. Ergonomic and environmental considerations will also play their part

Doyen of the British diesel engine, the hand assembled Gardner has gone modern with the 6LXC. Beautiful sculpture

ABOVE: *Perkins turbocharged, in-line T6.3544 diesel compared with Scania's apparently complicated but very neat turbocharged six* below

The Rolls-Royce C range engine (this one is the C6200G) shows the turbocharger's rotor

Perkins big V8 540 diesel without turbocharger

Detroit Diesel have the Silver series; V6-92 with turbocharger

turbocharged diesels are becoming available after a long period of painstaking development, very much the Gardner way of doing things.

Equally famous in the world of diesels is the name of Perkins of Peterborough, though, like Gardner, Perkins have been predominantly occupied with producing a range of truck engines with a top power output rather below that required for 32 tonners and upwards. Perkins started building diesels in 1932 when the price of derv was 5d per gallon (petrol was 1s 4d) and rapidly became the biggest producer of oil engines in the world. The firm prospered until the late fifties but after making its first financial loss and losing its founder, Frank Perkins, on his retirement, it became part of the Massey Ferguson Group, which itself promptly got into difficulties which are yet to be resolved. Like some other engine builders, Perkins adopted the compact vee cylinder formation and, like them, had some difficulty in getting it right. It obviously came right in the end as the V540, a ninety degree V8 of 9 litres capacity is currently a popular choice for artic tractors in the 22 to 28 ton GCW classes.

Of more importance to the makers of the biggest trucks are the activities of a relative newcomer to the automotive diesel scene in Britain, Rolls-Royce Motors Ltd. This is the title of the part of the original Rolls-Royce whole which escaped, or, rather, did not need the helping hand of the National Enterprise Board after the catastrophic financial collapse of 1971. The first Rolls-Royce diesel engine rumbled into life in 1949 but it was not until 1966 that the Eagle range was offered to the makers of premium trucks. The automotive unit was based on the C range of industrial engines which, ironically, were being made in the old Sentinel works in Shrewsbury, birthplace of so many of the famous steam wagons. The story of the Eagles well illustrates the development process which the truck maker has to do for himself if he insists on manufacturing his own major components. Both the C and Eagle ranges are based on 6 in. by 5 in. cylinder dimensions which give a swept volume of two litres. This gives some idea of the scale of the diesels tucked away beneath the premium cabs where a single cylinder can have a cubic capacity as great as or greater than that of all four in the average medium sized car engine. Twenty five years of development has seen this significant two litres yielding successive increases of power to the extent that output has doubled in that time. In the light of recent energy history it seems probable that this success in extracting sheer power is less important than the salient fact that the increase in efficiency during the quarter century has made the cost per horse power three times cheaper in real terms. This is the sort of advance which makes the world's oil reserves effectively very much bigger.

At the very outset, the Rolls C range had been designed for pressure charging, so the very first Eagles were all turbocharged except for the 220 bhp version which was allowed to breathe naturally. RR engineers claim that the heavy end of the British market, at present the trucks hauling 28 to 32 tons, needs power plants producing at least 265 bhp and this can be extracted from the Mark III Eagles at engine speeds as low as 1900 rpm with benefits in economy and lower wear and noise levels.

Few manufacturers impress upon watchers as to what engine a particular truck uses. Daf are an obvious exception. Who can be sure what's in these?

LEFT: *This Seddon Atkinson is running a Rolls-Royce diesel here just off the M1 motorway. This manufacturer is proud of the association*

Looking ahead, the company claims that it is ready for the long awaited increase in permitted weights to around 40 tons for which the Eagle 290L is said to be ideal. Rolls are also big in military diesels and the same two litre cylinder enables a V12 tank engine to develop over 600 horse power. Leyland, Foden, ERF and Seddon-Atkinson all offer their customers the option of having a Rolls-Royce beneath the cab floor. A Foden fitted with an Eagle diesel has been evolved as a specimen quiet heavy vehicle. In conjunction with the Transport and Road Research Laboratory the difficulties of encapsulating a truck power plant have been tackled. The results in terms of noise suppression proved to be excellent, the serious problems arise when the casings required interfere with servicing and engine cooling.

All the truck makers mentioned above offer Cummins engines as alternative to the Rolls. After a somewhat chastening experience with big V8s, Cummins are now in the forefront of in-line 6 cylinder design, running neck and neck with RR. The American parent company of Cummins began building diesels in the early thirties and eventually set up in Britain in 1956. Shotts in Lanarkshire is where the six cylinder models are built and these 14 litre units have followed a similar development path to the diesels produced in Shrewsbury. The Cummins units are unusual in employing four valves per cylinder to get the air in and the exhaust gases out, as well as fuel injectors which are positively operated by the engine's main camshaft. The 'big cam' is a feature of the E series, designed very much with economy in mind just like the Rolls L series. Ouputs of 290, 350 and 370 bhp are attained by the three members of the E series, all of which are turbocharged. In the smallest of the Es,

Even motorway inclines like this require maximum power to enable a truck to maintain speed. Looks like the Mercedes is catching that ERF. Power is never plentiful enough

pressure charging is used more to control accurately the burning of the fuel than to boost power output. The E350 and E370, have their power boosted by being fitted with after coolers. Intercoolers, after coolers, charge coolers, all these are different names for the same thing. They are, in fact, heat exchangers using either air or water flows to lower the temperature of the air issuing from the turbocharger. As the air cools its density increases, thus enabling each cylinder to take in a greater weight of charge and hence produce more power. A secondary gain achieved by charge cooling is the reduction of heat stresses in the cylinder heads and block. Though Cummins claim that these are 'drivers' engines', mainly because they are very flexible, the firm has gone to the trouble of producing a handbook outlining the driving technique required to get the best out of their E series.

Subscribing totally to the Ford philosophy of buying in all the major components, ERF, Britain's only surviving independent maker of premium trucks, offers a wider range of engine options than the multi-national company. These come from Rolls-Royce, Gardner and Cummins, axles are bought from GKN, Eaton and Rockwell, gearboxes from Eaton Fuller and ZF. A mile or two away on the same road running out of the small town of Sandbach in Cheshire lies the Foden factory, until recently owned by an independent company like ERF. Founded by members of the same family (ERF are the initials of Edwin Richard Foden) the two Cheshire firms have long fought each other as well as unrelated competitors to keep their respective shares of the same market. Foden bought in all their engines from the same sources as ERF, but persisted until the eleventh hour in making their own gearboxes, axles

Mercedes-Benz have been using their own diesels. No need to reinforce that message with the familiarity of the three-pointed star

and even clutches. In 1980 the independent Foden story sadly came to an end. Fodens Ltd., became the Sandbach Engineering Company, a subsidiary of Paccar Inc., American builders of Kenworth and Peterbilt trucks. The current Foden Fleetmaster tractor units are offered with a choice of Rolls-Royce or Cummins Engines, Lipe-Rollway twin plate clutch, Fuller gearbox and Rockwell hypoid bevel rear axle, very much a collection of prime components.

With Seddon-Atkinson, an Oldham, Lancs., company now part of the US International Harvester Group, predictably also wedded to the idea of buying in most of the major components, this leaves only Leyland in Britain manufacturing both engines and premium trucks, somewhat of a contrast to what goes on in Europe. Seddon fit either Rolls-Royce or Cummins power plants driving through nine speed Fuller gear boxes to hub reduction axles of their own make. Judging by reports of its excellent showing in the T45, the Leyland TL12 Flexitorque diesel exclusively powering the first Roadtrains gives little away to the power plants developed by the engine specialists. Nevertheless, Leyland customers now have the choice, as they always have since the birth of the Marathon, so the Rolls-Royce Roadtrain is available for operators in love with the Eagle 265L. Likewise, Cummins fanciers can still have their latest Leyland propelled by an E290. Like the Marathon, the T45 series has power plants connected to a Leyland hub reduction rear axle via American designed clutches and gearboxes from Spicer and Eaton Fuller.

BELOW: *Ford have tried to assemble the best possible components into one truck series. The Transcontinental range is the result. Cummins engine for this semi-custom rig*

General Motors, the American parent of Bedford, big in Britain's medium truck market though not so big in the premium field, builds the Detroit Diesel, unusual in being a positively blown two stroke. Many truck enthusiasts will remember the aircraft-like drone of the old Commer diesel two strokes, the sort of noise calculated to raise the hackles of all but the hardest hearing environmentalists. Detroit two stroke diesels are vee engines, either with the six or eight cylinders each one of 71 cu. in. capacity (1164 cc), hence the designations 6V-71 or 8V-71. The latter develops nearly 300 bhp and powers the heaviest of the Bedford TM range. TM tractor models are classified according to the designed GCW in kilogrammes divided by ten, hence the TM3800 has a GCW of 38,000 Kg. or 38 tonnes. On trucks where the Vauxhall badge has survived on the front panel, the model number is displayed in small characters below the winged figure. The TM3800 can also be bought with a Cummins E290 as prime mover. Constant mesh gearboxes by Eaton Fuller and Spicer connect the engines to double reduction Eaton spiral bevel axles. Relatively recently, a four stroke Detroit Diesel was born and it seems unlikely that the two stroke will survive all the four stroke competition.

The Ford philosophy that spawned the Transcontinental is totally rejected in the land which spearheaded the invasion of this country by a new breed of truck. There is no doubt that the two Swedish commercial vehicle makers, Scania and Volvo, have changed the face of European trucking, and increasingly this means world trucking. The first Scanias came to Britain in 1967 and first year registrations amounted to only a

LEFT: *General Motors promote the sales of their 'captive' Detroit Diesel engines. This Bedford TM has left the fold for a Cummins turbo engine*

150. Now the Scania population on British roads is estimated at 11,000 vehicles, most of them in the heavyweight class. Scania claim, however, that their very successful operation in Britain has not hit domestic industries all that hard as every Scania made incorporates a considerable proportion of British parts. These certainly do not include major components like engines, gear boxes and axles, as all these are Scania designed and Scania made. The range of engines begins with an 8 litre turbocharged in-line six, followed by a similar 11 litre unit also exhaust blown and developing a hefty 280 bhp. Top of the range is a 14 litre V8 with no less than 388 horsepower on tap. Gearboxes by Scania are all-synchromesh with 10 speeds obtained by range-changing or splitting the basic five ratios. There is a wide choice of final drives, the all-Scania axles including single and double reduction spiral bevel and hypoid types.

Volvo are even more emphatic about the rightness of designing and making every component to complement every other, claiming that the

Seddon Atkinson introduced the 401 as a premium tractive unit but to a lightweight specification. Fitting alloy wheels takes off a surprising amount of weight

key to all aspects of successful truck operation lies in the correct matching of the driveline to the vehicle and to the type of work expected of it. Like Scania, Volvo staunchly stick to all-synchromesh gearboxes and use both range changers and splitters to provide up to sixteen ratios. The engines which drive through these boxes are all in-line sixes of 7, 10 and 12 litres capacity, hence the well-known model numbers — F7, F10 and F12. For a long time very much the leading advocate of the value of turbocharging, the marque began using forced induction as long as 25 years ago, and is noted now for the extraction of high outputs from relatively small cubic capacities. This is rather the reverse of the current Cummins approach and one which is very dependent on intelligent driving if the fuel mileage is to be stretched to the limit. The F86 and F88 won the make much of its popularity in Britain and earned their almost legendary reputation by proving to be almost boringly reliable and extremely comfortable to drive, in fact setting a completely new dimension in cab comfort. The Volvo cab certainly had all the competition falling over itself making valiant efforts to find new ways of inspiring driver loyalty, something that many of the established truck makers had not thought very much about in the past. Volvo are still setting a hot pace in this respect by offering full cab air conditioning as standard feature in both F10 and F12 models; no other truck sold in Britain offers this. Of more direct interest to operators is the first ever scheme to give a factory-backed warranty on used Volvos valid for six months or 30,000 miles. Like Scania, Volvo are always at pains to point out that the balance of trade between this country and Sweden is in Britain's favour, and besides being a good customer of British industry, Volvo actually have a truck and bus manufacturing plant at Irvine in Scotland, so many of their vehicles are at least as British as a Bedford or Ford.

The Dutch manufacturer, Daf, also will have nothing to do with outside engine builders, basing the range on two in-line six cylinder diesels of 8.25 and 11.6 litres capacity. Again, a relatively high output is obtained relative to swept volume with intercoolers being used to boost the power of two of the members of the all turbocharged line up. The gearboxes do, however, come from external sources, ZF supplying both synchromesh and constant mesh transmissions while constant mesh only boxes come from Eaton Fuller. Daf, however, make the axles and all those fitted to the heavyweights have double reduction final drives.

Mercedes, again, stick strictly to engines and axles of their own design and manufacture. Employing a modular principle to provide units of varying capacities, Mercedes diesels are built in V6, V8 and V10 configurations giving swept volumes of approximately 10, 13 and 16 litres. For some reason or other, the German manufacturer has lagged appreciably in the application of turbocharging, but in view of developments elsewhere in the all-important matter of fuel economy the value of staying mainly with naturally aspirated engines seems to be in considerable doubt. A recent shift in Daimler-Benz policy has been the adoption of constant mesh gearboxes supplied by Eaton Fuller. Before then the chief outside supplier was ZF and synchromesh ruled.

Unique in the European truck world in fitting air cooled engines exclusively, another German maker, Magirus Deutz, is part of a conglomerate known as Iveco (Industrial Vehicles Corporation) in which the Italian vehicle manufacturing giant, Fiat, has a very big stake. The Italian designers, like almost all the others in the business, prefer to cool their pots with water. So, although Maggies (the popular name for MD over here) and Fiats are now look-alikes, the similarity ends abruptly when the cabs are tilted. Magirus claims that its V8 and V10 diesels, built up from modules like Mercedes-Benz power units, score significantly on reliability due to the absence of perishable hoses and other water escape routes, pointing out that as many as 40 per cent of all truck breakdowns involve the conventional water cooling system. The naturally aspirated Deutz powerplants come from KHD (Klockner-Humboldt-Deutz) another member of Iveco, and produce 260 bhp in V8 form, the V10 giving out as much as 320 bhp. Experiments are afoot which could prove that air cooling facilitates the encapsulation necessary to cut engine noise to an absolute minimum, just as Magirus claims it does. The doubters of the value of air cooling might well point to what happened to the VW Beetle. ZF figure in yet one more maker's products by supplying Magirus with gearboxes, these having their ratios multiplied by splitters or range-changers, or both.

Fiat engines, in contrast to those of its partner, are water cooled, quite orthodox diesels and the Italians have not been particularly quick to appreciate the benefits to be gained from forced induction. All engine production is in-house, the range including in-line sixes of 10.6 and 13.8 litres capacity as well as a massive 90 degree V8 disposing of no less than 17 litres. Fiat-made 10 speed splitter gearboxes link the smaller engines to Fiat double reduction axles, but all the V8 power is transmitted through 13 speed Eaton Fuller boxes. The lastest news from Iveco indicates that both Magirus and Fiat have now joined the exhaust-driven induction club and made consequent gains in maximum power outputs.

Very quick off the mark with turbocharged petrol engines, for both ordinary passenger and Formula 1 racing cars, Renault also manufacture their own turbocharged diesels in the guise of 12 litre in-line sixes, the more powerful of which have an air-to-air system to cool the induction air. Until fairly recently, the trucks now produced under the Renault umbrella carried either the Berliet or the Saviem name and the Berliet hub reduction axle features in the current range while the gearboxes are bought in from either ZF or Eaton Fuller.

Maschinenfabrik Augsburg Nuremberg, otherwise German truck maker Man, like Mercedes, have now begun to take constant mesh gearboxes from Eaton Fuller who therefore join ZF as an outside source for a major component. Man, however, build their own engines and offer both naturally aspirated and turbocharged units. The biggest one is a 16 litre V10 which manages to produce well over 300 horsepower without the aid of a blower. Smaller Man diesels are straight sixes which are either allowed to breathe straight from the atmosphere or through a turbo. The latter are given much-needed extra beef low down in the rev range by an induction layout tuned to bounce air into the cylinders, a classic method for improving engine breathing at low piston speeds.

10 Maintenance means replacement

No use at all . . . ruinous immobility . . . cleaning time . . . trouble on the road . . . sad image . . . swiftly approaching penury . . . easy routine checks . . . with the cab tilted . . . back to the factory . . . annual tests . . . driver as monitor . . . the little things . . . no consumerism.

Downtime is no use at all to the truck operator. It is then that his enormously expensive lump of machinery is standing doing nothing, active only in costing money instead of earning it. Road vehicles capable of running indefinitely without requiring regular servicing and irregular repairing have not yet been devised, or ever will be unless some miraculous way of preventing wear and deterioration can be discovered. Even then, accidents causing sufficient damage to keep a truck off the road will still happen.

According to the Road Haulage Association, in 1980 a 32 ton gross artic cost its owner no less than £18,000 per year when simply standing still. The standing charges, in fact, amounted to more than half of the total annual running cost of £30,000. For the sake of argument, the latter must be regarded as a somewhat conservative estimate as it was based on an annual mileage of only 40,000, and few long haul trucks cover as little as that in a year, so the standing charges must form a slightly smaller proportion of the total. Downtime, however, is inevitably more expensive than simple standing time. Then there are all the standing charges to pay plus labour and material costs for routine maintenance, for damage and mechanical repairs, and ultimately, perhaps for the near ruinous replacement of an engine or a cab.

The sheer size of a heavyweight artic tractor and that of its individual components means that the cost of working on it is far from negligible. Apart from the topping up of the fuel tank, a far from brief task when there is up to 60 gallons (sometimes more) to pump in, the simplest essential maintenance job is keeping clean the windscreen, side and rear windows, mirrors and lamps. A conscientous driver will get to work unfailingly on these at every halt during dirty weather, and in Britain there often does not seem to be any other kind. So the time spent on keeping vital visibility completely intact can take up a far from negligible slice of every working day. Cleaning just the windscreen involves climbing up on to not very adequate footholds in or on the front bumper and rubbing away at something like twenty square feet of greasy, mud or salt spattered glass. Smaller in area but just as important in the 'see and be seen' way of driving, the rear lamps are all of fifty feet away, not exactly a walk in the marathon class yet far enough to consume valuable minutes every time this essential journey is made. It is obviously difficult to determine how cost-effective refinements like headlamp washing equipment can be, but clearly under very bad conditions there can be no doubt of its enormous safety value.

Trouble on the road means inevitable downtime with the possible added sting of having to meet considerable recovery costs. The restrictions on driving and overall duty hours make accurate scheduling difficult enough and a relatively short, unscheduled stop on the hard shoulder can have dire consequences when time is running out. Any stop, however brief, where the truck concerned is causing traffic congestion and possible danger does very obvious harm to the industry's already sad image. Fortunately, the vehicle manufacturers recognise the importance of round-the-clock help which is available seven days a week, and appear to have spent some time in coining slick titles for the roadside services they offer their customers. Most explicit is the one used by Renault . . . Help! Daf's Dafaid and Scania's Lifeline echo the same sentiment. More staid but still expressive is Leyland's Co-driver, Bedford's Roadcall, Volvo's Action Volvo and Mercedes' Trans-Europe. Seddon-Atkinson came up

Heavy wrecking is a specialised job. This is a custom built wrecker on Bedford TM3800 components. Most use 'trade' plates only

with a more aggressive symbol, apparently derived from the initials SA, which were lengthened to Sabre. The bigger fleets can naturally provide a good deal of self-help in the shape of their own recovery services, but the plight of an owner-driver stuck at the roadside can be pretty grim, even if he can push to the back of his mind the fact that his cash flow has also come to a dead stop, or rather is flowing too swiftly in the direction of penury.

If roadside help cannot get a stricken tractor back on to the earnings trail, a substitute can take over the semi-trailer, thus minimising the disaster suffered irrevocably by the owner of a broken down, fully loaded rigid truck. Once back in the workshops, the tractor scores again over the rigid by occupying so much less of the always scarce floor space and fitting easily on to a hoist of relatively modest dimensions and load capacity. Not much can be seen of a big truck's power unit until the cab has been tilted. In the interests of reducing the time absorbed by the normal daily maintenance tasks and of eliminating the temptation to skip these jobs, some service points are accessible when the cab is still in the running position. These usually include the engine oil dipstick, oil and

This Ford Transcontinental wrecker is even more fancy. Not only does it have towing ability but it can also lift some vehicles off the road to then pull them without the conventional boom

water fillers, hydraulic reservoirs for clutch and power steering, and the windscreen washer tank, all reached through the front panel or grille. Nowadays, electrical fuses mostly live inside the cab.

With the cab tilted forward (usually by pumping up a hydraulic ram) to an angle of 60 to 70 degrees, the mechanics are in the relatively happy position of having to deal with what is virtually a bare chassis. This does not mean that everything is very easy to get at, though the DIY car owner will envy the way in which it is possible to work from above as well as from below. It will come as no surprise to anyone involved in maintaining smaller vehicles that straightforward replacement of components is now favoured rather than the fitting of new or refurbished parts to the used components. Simple economics dictate against the extensive dismantling of either major or minor units as this is now a very expensive way of doing things. Even in the days when stripping everything down to the last washer was the rule rather than the exception, and when every mechanic consequently knew what was inside the casing of every component, accurate diagnoses were very elusive and protracted investigations could be terrifyingly costly. The growth of complete component replacement has, of course, robbed workshop staffs of the vital opportunity to acquire

ABOVE: *British customising is very mild compared with that in North America. Maybe it's the weather. Here is a minimal modification. Ford have been encouraging owner-drivers and companies to buy more specialised components, witness the air horns and sun visor*

RIGHT: *Sophisticated rearward viewing. This heavy duty mirror from Trico-Folberth comes equipped with its own wiper, something more effective than the simple deflectors often fitted to cab corners*

and exercise diagnostic ability and thus accelerated the process of transferring engineering skills from the repair shop back to the maker's factory.

In most fleets, annual or set mileage overhauls are no longer undertaken, though the yearly roadworthiness tests persuade most operators to check all the test items in advance. The check list is over 60 items long, and submitting time after time a vehicle that is obviously suffering from poor maintenance can lead to the withdrawal of a licence to operate. In between annual tests it is possible for the lax operator to fall foul of a roadside spot check. But regular inspection of wearing parts not directly related to safety is no longer profitable. Maybe it never was; even when operating and workshop conditions were very different it must always have been something of a luxury to strip down a unit just to confirm that specified wear limits had or had not been reached. Current practice is to replace only when very definite symptoms indicate that it is necessary, otherwise to leave well alone. There is no certain way of knowing how long a particular component will last. Trucks engaged on similar duties may exhibit similar wear rates or quite differing ones. Clearly the drivers have something to do with this and probably constitute the most important variable, though equally clearly there are very many others.

A truly professional trucker is the most effective monitor of his vehicle's health, a truism that is not always accepted by workshop staffs, though the best ones do appreciate that he can be their most invaluable ally. They know that ignoring reported minor faults can lead to big trouble later. The truck manufacturers naturally play their part in the never-ending all-round efforts to reduce downtime, although some workshop managers claim that not enough is being done to prolong the life of obviously expendable parts like driving belts. Jobs such as fan belt renewal are said to come round too often, the resulting downtime costing infinitely more than the price of the failed or worn out component. The demise of the dynamo still appears to be mourned by those technicians who can remember it, especially when they happen to be employed in a workshop bedevilled by a spate of alternator failures. Wiring looms that make the separation of individual wires difficult are also much disliked.

There is no escape from the periodic replacement of normal wearing parts such as brake and clutch linings and the latest truck designs aim to expand the intervals between relining as far as possible. The move towards constant mesh gearboxes probably has much to do with their reputedly superior durability over the synchromesh types. One of the problems facing small operators, particularly, is the impossibility of gaining sufficient experience of all the options on offer. The type of consumerism which collects information on a wide range of operating experience covering the more popular private cars is never likely to be seen in the truck world. There it would inevitably turn out to be an enormously expensive project and one that the users would never be able to finance, even if they wanted to, and this is more than somewhat doubtful in an industry conducted mainly by fiercely independent characters.

11 'Knights of the Road'

Not knights now . . . first real test . . . folk tales . . . clear of trouble . . . no three-pointers . . . venturesome motorists . . . brakes first . . . just the beginning . . . arduous battle . . . buck passed . . . off the edge . . . backing on . . . no company . . . changing relationships . . . constant custodian . . . rivers with waves . . . mindless antics . . . unskilled labour . . . slightly euphoric . . . importance of feet.

It is a long time now since the accolade 'Knights of the Road' was bestowed on heavy vehicle drivers by one of the pop newspapers of the day. In those days the majority of the general populace had no experience whatsoever of driving any sort of vehicle, apart perhaps, from a push bike. So maybe it was easy for them to be persuaded that the man high in the cab was some sort of super being fighting with consummate skill and courage to control his rattling, roaring monster. In keeping with this image, he was always supposed to be chivalrously aware of all the lesser beings scurrying about on the ground below, so much so that he thought nothing of carefully stopping his truck in a village high street, then climbing down from aloft just to escort a child or an old lady across the road. Back in his cab again, he would always give way to the buses and trams that served then as everyman's private car; it did seem strange, though, that everyone seemed to sense somehow that truck and bus drivers were for ever at each others' throats. Maybe it was because the truck driver always got the bouquets for following funeral processions,

Conventional American Mack is a very rare beast in Europe. This Spanish registered rig comes with offset cab and few home comforts. It's hard to park in right hand drive Britain

carnivals and other parades without showing obvious signs of impatience. At least, that is how the popular newspapers apparently saw him.

Despite all this generally favourable publicity, the public's interest was never seriously aroused and the job of the truck driver failed signally to attract the sort of kudos that had made every other male child want to be a railway engine driver, or so it has always been said. Much more plausible is the theory that this was a myth created by rail-struck adults in an attempt to cover up their apparent retarded development. But there is nothing mythical about the consuming impatience with which virtually every teenager, male or female, living in the developed countries of the world, now waits for the day when he or she can get behind a steering wheel and drive on the open road. Not very many expressly want this to be the wheel of a truck, most are simply besotted by the prospect of being able to drive much lesser vehicles. But when finally they do succeed in getting a steering wheel into their hands, they find they have to begin to compete with each other and with the descendants of the old 'Knights of the Road' for a share of the promised road. There is no doubt that this sort of competition has made the lot of the modern professional driver very much harder and caused both the driving public as well as those citizens going about their business on foot to be much more critical of trucks and truck drivers. If they ever do feel admiration, it is only very begrudgingly.

More perhaps in the matter of driving than in any other skilled activity, familiarity definitely breeds contempt. Taking charge of a vehicle is something that almost everyone is allowed to do, and something that most amateur drivers do very badly, often to an extent which degrades the whole process. Many of the professionals are no better, but it has to be a sobering fact that the driver of a big artic in congested, narrow-streeted Britain must prove his skill time after time throughout the crowded hours of every working day if he is not going to leave behind him a trail of death and destruction. His first real test of skill comes on the day he takes his special driving test, a requirement originally instituted in 1934 when general driving tests began. Once again road transport was badly served by government after all testing was suspended on the outbreak of World War 2. Thirty years were to elapse before HGV testing was resumed. As if to make very belated amends, in 1969 driver training schools were set up under the aegis of the Road Transport Industry Training Board, thus establishing a system of HGV driver training and testing. Tuition had to be paid for by the pupils or their employers, the fees varying according to the class of licence aimed for. Currently a Class 3 licence covers rigid two-axled vehicles with a maximum gross weight of 16 tons. Class 2 additionally covers multi-axled rigids up to 30 tons MGW, whilst Class 1 also takes in all artics up to 32 tons MGW. In 1980 the ten day Class 1 course cost £600, scarcely peanuts even in such a rapidly melting currency as Sterling. Obviously, however, when the training vehicle has to be a top weight artic, just the running costs alone are bound to be high, and capital outlay and depreciation involve sums with several noughts attached.

The actual HGV test is carried out by senior examiners of the

*Typical American freeway where
big rigs have room to move.
Although speeds are supposed to be
low, efficiency is high. This Ford
9000 cabover with tanker has all
the road. Note factory paint and
CB aerials*

Department of Transport who work in much the same way as their colleagues engaged in testing fledgling car drivers. Thus the rules are much the same and the overall performance of the candidate is assessed as impartially as is humanly possible; there is no indulgence in any sort of trickery and the examiner expects to see a display of reasonable competence, not an exhibition of superhuman virtuosity. The initial aim of the training school's tuition is to rid pupils' minds of the well-established folk tales told about every type of driving test, tales peopled by examiners alleged to solicit bribes, or who are supposedly hell-bent on failing a candidate in order to be able to conform to some fanciful quota of failures. So an important part of the instruction is morale building. Aspirants to a Class 1 pass in particular are reminded often of its being a matter for pride, besides opening the way to the top of the profession.

With so much experience and expertise put into the process of instructing and testing drivers for all types of vehicle, it is a reasonable assumption that if everyone drove as instructed for the relevant test, road accidents would be almost unknown. The fully qualified artic driver, however, has to learn very quickly that safe driving skills are not enough. This applies almost as much to anyone piloting the biggest rigids, but even more so to the skipper of a drawbar trailer outfit, yet he is not required to have a Class 1 licence. Anomalies such as this never do seem to get ironed out. The fact remains that either alone or in combination with the driver of another Jumbo HGV, the artic driver can, by his own incompetence, effectively snarl up vast sections of built-up area, perhaps even the whole road system of a small town. At best he will merely slow everything down, at the same time making only very slow progress himself. At worst, he will block completely a main traffic artery, causing delay, disruption and other incompetent drivers to have their own, further disruptive accidents. Therefore he is taught to use his skill and experience to stay well clear of trouble, not as a means of extracting himself from trouble he should never have risked getting into in the first place.

Knowledgeable motorists getting acquainted with the training methods and general philosophy of the HGV courses soon recognise that they aim to teach what have come to be known as advanced driving techniques. These put the emphasis on educated observation of the action going on all around, and in particular of the happenings on the road ahead. The man at the wheel of a big truck is ideally situated for reading the road ahead of him and forecasting with considerable accuracy just what the state of play will be when he actually arrives where the action is. With fore-knowledge he can then aim to place his vehicle in the right attitude, to have it in the right gear, and to be travelling at the right speed . . . right, that is, for the prime purpose of moving his truck further on its intended journey as smartly as the rules of safety and courtesy will allow. If he is a stranger to the route, his powers of observation will have to be stretched to the limit if wrong slots are to be avoided; three point turns are rarely feasible for artics! The constant search for the clues that help him forecast developments allows no let-up of concentration. Among these are things like the bus with passengers preparing to get off,

BELOW: *Britain is cramped for space. Seldom is it possible to be out of sight of habitation even on a motorway. This Mercedes rig is about to escape across the Channel as it heads past Dover Castle*

RIGHT: *Heavy truck in the heart of Britain. No sleeper cab for this Foden driver as he crosses the Severn Bridge. The country is littered with drivers' digs for those who can't get home*

puffs of exhaust steam coming from a car at the kerb, a pedestrian with umbrella rampant pushing his way to the edge of the pavement, a child's ball rolling out of a side street. Fine, sure judgement is paramount to avoid any loss of momentum which always means unnecessary hard work for both driver and truck before it can be regained, not to mention the extra wear and tear on both and the waste of fuel.

Observation has to be just as perceptive of the scene behind the truck, and here the driver of an artic is at a considerable disadvantage when the semi-trailer is high sided. Not very many of his fellow road users appreciate that the giant-sized, efficient rear view mirrors invariably fitted to modern tractive units are fully effective only when tractor and trailer are in a straight line. As soon as the cab pivots, however slightly, relative to the trailer, some rearward vision is lost, the mirror then beginning to reflect an ever widening view of the body side. It is at times like this that stupidly venturesome motorists can creep unseen alongside the truck and only the acutely observant trucker will have been forewarned by the attitude of the car before it was lost from view.

This type of incident is clearly illustrated in films used for HGV driver training. So is another possible conflict with other vehicles where the sheer size of the truck demands the use of the whole of the particular carriageway to complete a manoeuvre. Again, correct anticipation is all that stands between the trucker and a total impasse with traffic brought to a prolonged standstill in every direction. When two artics are in conflict with neither able to move, both drivers are at fault because they have obviously ignored their training on correct positioning. Although a very natural emphasis is placed on the need to make satisfactory progress on every journey, the pupils do have it hammered into them that the brakes are there to be used, not just kept as a last resort. Steering a big truck out of a sudden emergency is simply not on except in the rarest of circumstances. The safer answer, therefore, is to stop or at least attempt to stop; swerving a 32 ton vehicle violently to avoid, say, a suicidal pedestrian, is likely to lead to a full scale disaster such as mowing down a bus queue or turning the whole rig over on top of passing motorists. If the load happens to be an explosive or toxic one even more horrific results could ensue.

Assuming that he manages to keep out of trouble during his open road journey, the artic driver is almost certain to have to face difficult manoeuvres at the end of it. Even the most anti-truck car driver has been heard to voice his admiration for the skill that slots a 50 ft long artic backwards down a walled-in passage very little wider than the distance between the outer edges of its mirrors. It is, in fact, all done by mirrors

BELOW: *Yugoslav registered, Italian built Fiat on a Belgian autoroute is typical of the road transport industry today. Luckily, driver standards are universally high. Trailer shows Italian habit of three axles but with only two having twin wheels*

RIGHT: *Slowing for the Aust toll booths on the English side of the Severn Bridge. This is an Irish registered Daf with big sleeper cab. Nothing unconventional*

and very often under the pressure of knowing that other traffic is waiting impatiently for the cab to finally creep clear of the roadway. The opposite lock technique necessary to place the trailer accurately where it is supposed to go is naturally one that has to be demonstrated in the test.

The acquisition of a Class 1 licence is, of course, just the beginning. Thereafter, only the driver with a self-critical approach and a determination not to make the same mistake twice will become truly first class. The best ones tend to make driving a way of life, taking enormous pride in the skills that have become vital to the maintenance of the way of life that citizens of the eighties have learned to expect. Those same citizens are seldom willing to accord him the status he deserves, yet the modern breed of truck, impressive solely in terms of sheer size yet fairly handsome with it, is winning more and more admiration from previously uninterested abservers. But only the knowledgable are aware of how much technology is changing this indispensable carrier of so much of the nation's merchandise.

For the truck driver, these changes have their plus and minus sides. Apart from everything else, in the days of not so long ago strong arms and even stronger legs were a prime requirement during the long hours spent at the wheel, so brawn always seemed to be much more important than brains. The latter could help, but if the flesh was unable. . . . A minor millenium came with the development of power assistance for all the major controls, forcing mere brawn to take a back seat. Compressed air began to provide the muscle that was once needed for booting out the clutch and bringing in the brakes, it also began to take the effort out of gear-changing and applying the parking brake. Best of all, hydraulic pressure came to the aid of the arms that had to turn the wheel and quickness added to lightness made steering at low speeds something approaching pleasure instead of the painfully slow, arduous battle it had once been.

Like everyone else travelling the open road in the sixties and early seventies, truckers did not give much thought to the possibility of the oil running out. Most operators have always had fuel costs on their minds ever since the coal burning days of the steam wagons, but it took the oil shortages of 1973, followed by all the subsequent alarums and excursions that sent the price spiralling ever upwards, to get things really moving on the diesel economy front. Somehow the engine builders began to boost efficiency quite significantly in each succeeding model. Turbocharging was the name of a relatively new game that made more and more power available from relatively old engines, the snag for the driver being that it was not quite as available as it had been. It could be extracted only by keeping engine revs inside a very narrow speed band, and brains as well as sixteen speed gearboxes began to be needed. So the buck was passed to the foot on the throttle or rather to the human computer controlling it, ever the vital link in the economy chain. If conducting a long haul truck safely and economically had not quite become an intellectual game, it had become an activity that demanded ten tenths concentration for ten tenths of every journey.

This applies particularly to the growing proportion of British truckers who spend a great deal of their professional lives steering down the wrong side of the road. Added to the normal hazards are the hassles and delays at frontier crossings and restrictive national laws like the German and French ones that impose trucking bans on Sundays and holidays. Combined with the limitations on driving hours, these can be highly frustrating for a driver thankfully scenting home after a protracted trans-continental haul. Some truckers are brave and enterprising enough to run regularly off the edge of Europe's road system and take to the dusty, desert tracks leading to the middle eastern states where so much of the oil comes from. Few of them belong to the generation whose alleged boyhood ambition was to drive a train, those who do must have realised that an engine driver would never get so far.

The days when most of the trucks crossing the seas had to be backed on or off the ferries are almost gone, Vehicle carrying ships have grown bigger and bigger and the adoption of bow doors has made roll-on, roll-off an apter description of what actually happens during loading and unloading. But if the ultimate destination lies across some less trafficked stretch of water, say on one of the Greek islands, then backing on is the rule and it has to be done inch by inch up a long ramp and into the relatively tiny floating garage. With his vehicle safely stowed below, the transcontinental trucker can relax until the time comes to get the outfit hauling itself back on to terra firma, or can he? Possibly, if he happens to be as good a sailor as he is a trucker. Otherwise, he is unlikely to get much in the way of relaxation when heavy seas batter his ship, a not infrequent occurence around these coasts.

To the employee truck driving can be simply a way of earning a living,

This flat bed semi has sophisticated lifting gear permanently installed. Local delivery efficiency is maintained but the haulier would lose out over very long distances

one that can last a lifetime or just as long as it takes to get into transport management. To the owner-driver it can, or rather, under present conditions, must be a whole way of life unless or until it serves as a stepping stone leading towards the creation of yet another new transport business. Whether employed or self-employed, the professional driver on long haul work spends a high proportion of his working hours on the move with no company but his own, and for many there has to be more in it than just a job. To be naturally good at it he has to possess an inbuilt mechanical sympathy in an age when destructive urges are becoming more and more prevalent, he has to be self-reliant in a society where habitual buck-passing is very much the applaudable norm, he must be wholly satisfied with his own company in a world where the natural loner is always more than slightly suspect.

But in some ways the isolation of that seat high up in the cab is more apparent than real. The open road is a place of constantly changing relationships that have to be brought to a satisfactory conclusion if mutual disasters are to be avoided. In North America the Citizens Band radio revolution has revealed how garrulous truckers can be, though it remains to be seen whether or not this is a strictly Stateside trait. But the loneliness of the long distance trucker can be as real as that of his counterpart on foot, peaking, perhaps, on sparsely populated stretches of night shrouded motorway. The autobahnen, autoroutes, autostrade, motorways, whatever these featureless routes are called, have added thousands of truly boring miles to the European network and boredom in the cab can be a very real enemy. In some regions, a varying terrain might seem like a good anitidote to the monotony, but motorways almost always keep the local scenery, however dramatic, at arm's length. And even where there are mountains, a trucker's life is dominated by the motorways, those broad rivers of tarmac and concrete that carry the lion's share of European freight rapidly towards its various destinations. From the height of the cab they look smooth enough, but they can be rivers with waves. Despite suspension seats and suspended cabs, the ride is distinctly hard, the best of sound damping fails to smother completely the roar of 300 bhp or so being generated beneath the cab floor, the undulating hiss and rumble of a dozen or more giant tyres resonates through springs and

Not quite sure whether that semi-trailer could be driven into the Boeing 747. Doubtful. However, the Leyland Roadtrain rig looks impressive even in company with giant aircraft. BRS obviously know how to advertise their wares

frame, pedals and steering wheel, rising and falling in pitch and volume as the road texture coarsens and fines. Life at a mile a minute is lived in far from pampered comfort, despite what the truck makers say. Enormous stamina is needed just to endure the long hours of unchanging sounds, of concentrating on a scene that is always changing yet always the same. Drowsiness can become an insidious enemy whose visits are revealed only when it retreats and wakefulness returns with a guilty start. Traffic patterns vary but the endless road does not, and there is often no way of knowing whether it is running across Berkshire, Bedfordshire or Staffordshire, or whether the soil of Germany or Holland, France or Italy lies beneath the asphalt.

Ford Cargo 'module' series. 1981 launch sees a takeover from the faithful D series. Cargo can go up in weight too although it is not designed for long distance work. That's reserved for the sleeper cab Transcontinental

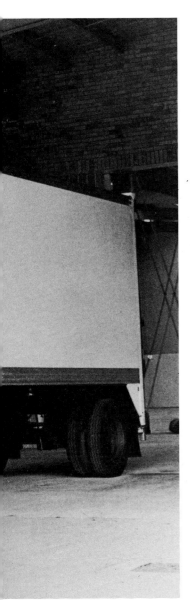

The only predictable variable is the weather, though this is not true of settled climates where the constant sun only adds to the monotony, providing change only by the shortening and lengthening of the shadows. Truckers confined to Britain are less likely to be bothered by the sun than by rain and fog. Rain provides both the lubricant that lengthens braking distances and the fog-like wheel spray which cuts vital visibility. Fog emphasises how lethal is the mix of cars and trucks and tragedy does not always single out only the occupants of the smaller vehicles. It is at its worst during the hours of darkness and then the accident rate soars. Very recent figures never exist, but in 1978 one hundred and seventy nine British truckers were killed on the road, and over ten thousand were injured, small figures, perhaps, in relation to the total road casualties, though far from insignificant ones in the context of the death and injury toll of workers generally reckoned to be in more dangerous occupations. The big EEC countries over the same period recorded proportionately more deaths and fewer injuries, possibly reflecting differences in road and traffic conditions.

Wherever he happens to be, the top weight truck driver bears a considerable weight of financial responsibility on his shoulders. Not only is he responsible for the safe passage of the biggest vehicle in regular use on the road, he is also the constant custodian of a dauntingly sizeable chunk of wealth. Even when returning to base with an unloaded suspension allowing the trailer bogie to hop from bump to bump, a moment's carelessness or incompetence can write off £30,000 or more of his boss's money, or at least send his insurance premium sky high. If he is an owner-driver, it will be his own pocket that suffers. This sort of sum, however, can pale into insignificance when compared with the possible total value of his fully laden artic. Twenty odd tons of gold bars would be an unlikely consignment, but a quite mundane load of washing machines can be the equal in value of one premium tractive unit, so there is nothing unlikely in the man with his foot on the throttle controlling the rolling destiny of hardware worth as much as a hundred grand.

Members of other professions which are more prestigious in the eyes of a not very discerning public might care to reflect on whether or not a few brief moments of inefficiency, whether caused by fatigue, an indulgent spell of wool gathering, or the understandably bloody minded reaction to the mindless antics of the fools about them, could produce the dire consequences that can face a truck driver guilty of similar errors and omissions. If they are to be truthful, they must admit that driving a desk will only very rarely, if ever, be subject to such risks and will almost certainly be better paid. What is more, the trucker at work is isolated to a degree that the man on the footplate, flight deck or bridge is not, while the often continuous string of emergencies encountered impact his consciousness at a rate seldom experienced on rails, in the air or on water.

Fortunately there are signs that top weight drivers are managing to improve their status; more and more they are being consulted about the merits or otherwise of the various vehicles on the market for the job in hand. Not so many years ago this would have been almost unthinkable. It is only since the manufacturers began to seriously consider the comfort and safety of the driver that the latter has had some sort of yardstick with which to measure how much a particular maker was doing for him. One of the first firms to cash in on driver-appeal was far-seeing Volvo. The Swedish maker recognised that noise, road shocks, extreme heat and cold could make the lot of the trucker a far from happy one, even when he was at the wheel of an otherwise sound and reliable design. Very much to the point was Volvo's expressed concern about the effect of unrefined, uncomfortable machines on the status of the profession. Someone once said of the conventional gearbox that 'it was brutal but it worked'. The same sentiment could have been applied truthfully to even the best trucks of the far from remote past. Driving them was so very much a test of strength and stamina that the job was regarded as unskilled or semi-skilled labour best left to the direct descendants of the long distance carter of the pre-railway days. Unfortunately, even the premium trucks of today can be operated, apparently quite satisfactorily, by unthinking drivers equipped only with the manual dexterity needed to maintain control. Efficiency rates not at all, and it is easy to see why. Millions of car drivers continually demonstrate that there is nothing instinctive or naturally rewarding in making fuel go far. The truck driver, faced with maintaining schedules that may or may not have been drawn up with fuel economy in mind and without the sanction of having to dip into his own pocket to keep his tanks topped up, is unlikely to develop into a skilled economist when he is such a natural spendthrift in his car.

Volvo, and some other manufacturers and interested organisations, have conducted tests which demonstrate quite conclusively how economy-trained drivers can boost mpg whilst maintaining the sort of progress that adds little of significance to journey times. Also illustrated was how training concerned with fuel-stretching produced the mentality which then began to concern itself with other aspects of economical operation. But too often in Britain operators choose to ignore the fact that the newly fledged Class 1 driver, slightly euphoric about achieving a first time pass enlarging both his working horizons and possible pay, has merely satisfied the examiner of his ability to get his artic from A to B in reasonable safety. The man from the DoT will not have noted which of the gears should have been engaged to keep engine revs and throttle opening at the level demanding the minimum possible flow of fuel through the injectors. As for the understandably nervous examinee, nothing of this will have entered his head. His employer, pleased by the prospect of having another man qualified to move as much as 20 tons in one haul might momentarily consider having him taught the rudiments of driving frugally but the thought is unlikely to be translated into action. Which is odd, really, since so many operators have bowed to the necessity of improving their drivers' work environment, thus accepting the not negligible cost of more comfortable cabs and the consequent weight penalty which is going to go on draining their pockets throughout the life of the truck. When will they finally acknowledge the economic importance of their drivers' right feet? This would, at least, help them to get their money back and at the same time do a vital oil conservation job.

12 Log sheet to tachograph

Undoubted chore . . . a lying jade . . . Teutonic invention . . . stubborn Brits . . . a degree of automation . . . no absolute guarantee . . . the longer the safer?

For something like 50 years the British truck driver has been required by law to keep a written record of his working activities. This undoubted chore has always been justified by authority in the cause of controlling driving hours, a safety measure that few people will want to quarrel with. Like so many of the things regulated by statute, however, its workings tend to penalise those individuals with a sense of responsibility in often vain attempts to catch out the irresponsible types. Filling in the so-called log sheets was always a task hated by the majority of truckers, although the long haul men obviously had a better chance of being able to provide an accurate record of their working day than those with schedules complicated by multiple drops separated by shortish spells of driving. In these circumstances it was inevitable that the doctoring of log sheets became an integral part of a driver's day. This does not mean, necessarily, that there were widespread breaches of the law which had to be covered up. More often than not the sheets were filled in from memory, and

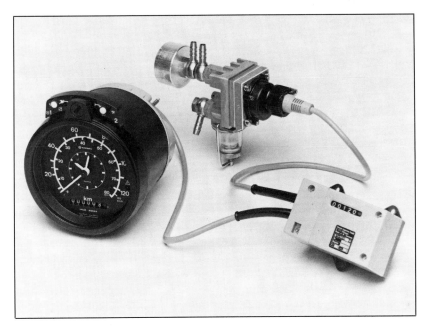

Components of the Lucas Kienzle automatic tachograph. There's also a fuel flow meter and cumulative counter on the right of the tachograph itself

memory can be a lying jade, especially when the mind has been concentrating on other things and involved in taking decisions which have to be 100 per cent correct for most of the time if the driving and the form filling is to continue. Worst of all, though, was the not unknown situation requiring a driver to falsify his records just to keep his employer out of trouble.

Somewhat ironically in the light of subsequent history, the device that was eventually to put a stop to all this difficult and devious form-filling was invented before the log sheet routine was imposed on British truckers. In 1927 the Germans invented the instrument now known as the tachograph, but even the mechanistically minded fatherland made little use of it in trucks until 1953 when it became a manadatory fitting to all goods vehicles with a maximum gross weight exceeding 7.5 tonnes. Meanwhile the conservative British had come to know and hate the tachograph no less than the log sheets and someone had coined the emotive phrase 'spy in the cab' to describe how the majority of drivers were alleged to feel about it. By 1970 the German lead had been followed by the EEC, and Britain, as a member of the Community, should have made the tachograph a compulsory fitment by 1976. But the stubborn Brits were not to give in easily. It finally took a European Court judgement to bring compulsion to this country though by then this was nothing new to British truckers employed on international haulage. Despite some threats of industrial action by the unions, the general transfer from log sheets to tachos was to happen peacefully in stages with the final stage completed by the end of 1981. There was no escaping the considerable cost which was estimated to be upwards of £200 million, a sizeable burden for transport operators and at the same time a nice, fat windfall for the several makers of the instrument.

The tachograph is basically a recording speedometer (*takhos* is Greek for speed) and the face it presents to the driver is that of a conventional instrument with the road speed indicated by a needle and the distance covered by a digital display. The dial also includes a normal clock face and hands, just as many ordinary speedometers do. In the case of the tachograph, however, the clock is an integral part of the mechanism. This is because its prime function is to produce a continuous recording of the day's work, so time is of the essence. The time spent driving, the time spent resting, the time spent on work activities other than driving, the speed of the vehicle at any particular time, the distance covered in a particular time, all these are recorded in the form of a graphical trace on a circular chart. Though much of the operation of the tachograph is automatic, regular human intervention has to see that the correct activity is being recorded. A single, multi-position switch has to be turned to the appropriate mode as indicated by international-type symbols. Through this the driver states whether he is driving, engaged in other either active or passive work, or simply resting. So there is still plenty of scope for involuntary or deliberate forgetfulness to distort what is supposed to be a true record. The Lucas Kienzle adds a little to the degree of automation by insisting on switching itself to the driving mode whenever the vehicle begins to move and switching back to 'other work' when it stops.

RIGHT: *In the cab – the Lucas Kienzle tachograph head is open with a chart being inserted*

BELOW: *'Unwritten' trucks somehow look suspicious. There's no good reason why they should, however. This Yugoslavian Fiat shows no signs of being anything other than legal and ready to run*

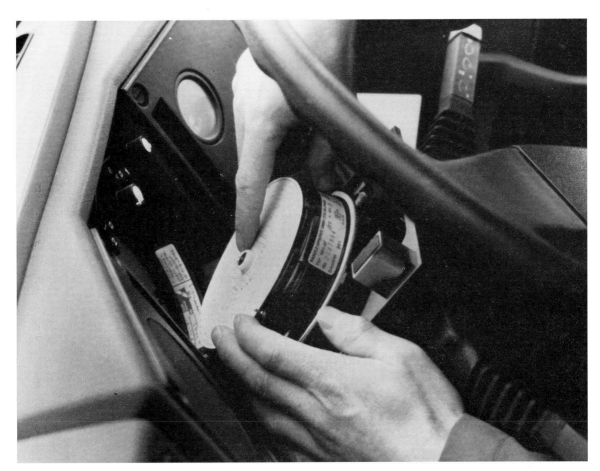

The law comes into all this only to ensure that there is no contravention of the driving hours regulations. Yet the tachograph cannot guarantee that injustices will not occur and less than careful programming is likely to see more problems raised than are supposed to have been solved. A driver taking his lawful rest, having set his tacho to the rest position, can find his apparently truthful recording accusing him of lawbreaking just because a shunter has had to move his truck only a yard or so. The chart does, of course, record whether or not the driver has been exceeding speed limits and there is no absolute guarantee that the trace on the tacho will not lead to him being prosecuted for speeding. His main safeguard, apparently, is that there are technical difficulties in the way of producing evidence that will stand up in court. One problem facing would-be prosecutors is that of trying to pin-point exactly where the alleged offence happened.

Sensible employers blessed with sensible drivers will, no doubt, not be slow in pointing out how fuel consumption jumps when a truck is going too fast, and some operators of large fleets claim that the tachograph has already boosted efficiency in almost every respect. Others tell lurid stories of the chronic unreliability of the controversial instrument, particularly of the drive mechanism. Everyone is faced with the cost of calibration every two years. One of the few certainties about the situation is the fact that owner drivers will not now be able to substitute stamina at the wheel for lack of organising time or ability. In theory this will mean few accidents caused by sheer fatigue, though even this issue has been thoroughly clouded by investigation results published in America. These were claimed to prove that the most accidents happen during the first hours of a driving stint. Moreover, the longer a driver stayed at the wheel, the more the accident rate decreased. This seems to be one of those instances where statistics can be made to prove anything. The truth may be that many drivers fail to 'drive themselves in' when starting a journey and hence are more accident prone than when their reactions have become properly attuned to the speed with which dangerous situations develop on the road.

13 A modern British heavy truck

Steady take-over . . . humanoid lorry . . . lame duck Leyland . . . rock bottom . . . instant success . . . self-testing diesels . . . most modern truck plant . . . little Lancashire town . . . the Spurriers in charge . . . complacency sets in . . . clean sheet of paper . . . nothing revolutionary . . . unprecedented testing . . . into the cold unsympathetic world . . . twelve months too late . . . in the great assembly hall.

Most of the people who can remember the inter-war years were children then. They were most likely quite unaware that the truck was steadily taking over the transporting of most of the nation's merchandise and normally applied the word 'truck' to the railway wagons which, even then, were being slowly but surely squeezed out of business. Trucks were known as 'lorries', just as they are now to most members of the lay population, while lorry drivers in their own parlance actually drove 'wagons'.

During those now far off days the author grew from infancy to adolescence, all the while observing automotive developments with a consuming interest that had reached a quite remarkable level well before the time came when he began to be shut away in the classroom to be made aware of the depressing fact that there was more to life than standing gazing avidly at the passing show of beautifully noisy, nicely smelly and satisfyingly huge lorries. Often it was insufficent for him just to stand and stare, and sometimes there was actually nothing to see. That was the time for a more active role to be adopted by actually becoming a lorry complete with the appropriate engine and gearbox noises. The smells were not so easy to engineer but most of these came from the steamers, and steam wagons were too quiet to be worth imitating very often. They lacked essential elements such as resonant, bellowing exhausts, gears that groaned, whined and screamed, cogs that clashed gutturally as the screaming slowly subsided.

It was no accident that the humanoid lorry was always a Leyland. Indoctrination had begun in the nursery when a picture book illustrating a Leyland six wheeler arrived from somewhere. From then on this was the king of lorries, the existence of other makes had to be acknowledged but only AEC and Scammell occasionally became rivals to be reckoned with. Later it was probably the Leyland Titan buses, petrol-engined still, and capable of putting on an electrifying performance up the long hills of West Yorkshire, which always tipped the scales in favour of the Lancashire-built vehicles. It did seem a pity, though, that Leyland was not in Yorkshire. The final decade before Hitler plunged the world into war saw the proliferation of the lightweight truck weighing less than $2\frac{1}{2}$ tons unladen because it was allowed to travel at no less than 30 mph. Ford and Bedford grew prosperous on it, Morris and Austin were never able to climb into the same league. Leyland replied with the Cub, but it seemed very much out of character, small in stature even when compared with rivals in its own class. So the name of 'Leyland' remained almost as much a synonym for 'heavy truck' as that of 'Kodak' was for 'camera'.

No-one then could possibly have foreseen how the once hallowed name was going to be dragged through the mire of political dissension. Lame duck Leyland was unthinkable, as was the application of the name to diminutive vehicles that any Tom, Dick or Harry could own and drive. But it happened. Lancashire's disastrous venture into the world of car manufacture has been publicised enough, so much so that the once famous name of Leyland rapidly became an infamous one. At one time, when the goings on in the Midlands car factories looked set to continue until the whole of the British motor industry sank without trace, a move was begun in Lancashire with the avowed intension of having the now dubious label jettisoned in favour of something completely different, and characterless, like BCV, or British Commercial Vehicles. Apparently the fact that the company's troubles really began as soon the word 'British' was added to 'Leyland Motor Corporation' must have been overlooked.

Fortunately it was finally decided to try to divest the cars of the name and to re-establish it as the honourable title of a celebrated truck. But it

BELOW: *Design studio drawings in the process of conceiving the Leyland Roadtrain. These were being processed during 1975*

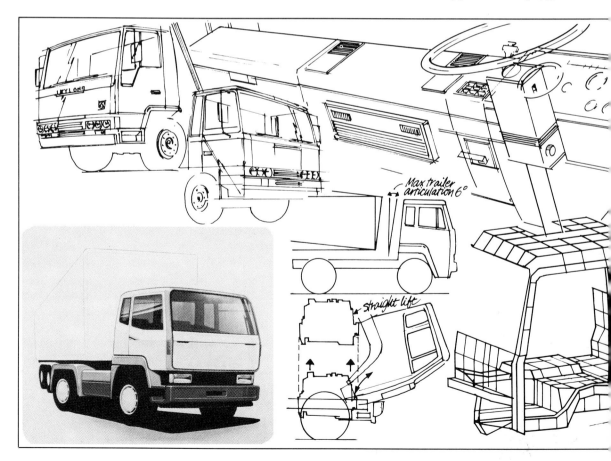

Built as long ago as 1968 this gas turbine powered Leyland 38 ton tractor showed enterprise. It was found to be far too thirsty even then

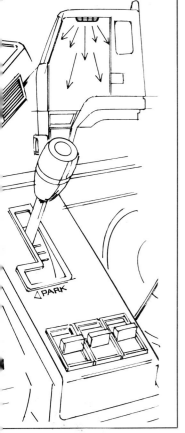

was not only Leyland's one-time impeccable reputation which had suffered damage. Just as serious was the draining off of financial resources to prop up the non-truck side of the conglomerate, thus bringing on a severe attack of investment deficiency at a time when it was most likely to prove fatal. To make things even more difficult, a very determined assault on the British truck market was being mounted by the main European manufacturers and as it prospered so the fortunes of Leyland sank further. The imports were able to make almost a clean sweep of the top weight field and the spotter totting up the number of Leyland artic tractors plying the trunk routes began to find them as rare as fine days in an English summer. They were well outnumbered by makes which a few years previously had been virtually unknown over here.

Rock bottom for Leyland was reached as the disastrous seventies were coming to an end, and the end for the marque could well have followed if the ensuing fight for survival had not been weaponed by the government. A fund of £350 million was made available for the much needed capital investment. Of this, £30 million were earmarked for the development of a new range of trucks intended to knock the imports for six. Another £32 million were to be spent on building an automated assembly plant for the new models. As the eighties arrived Leyland was beginning to have something to show for all this big spending, the new assembly plant coming partly on stream in mid 1980. Full commissioning was planned for the spring of 1981 when a fully computer controlled components store was due to start supplying both production lines to enable the designed capacity of 400 truck and bus chassis per week to be reached.

Meanwhile, the well-known law attributed to Murphy was to ensure that a world-wide recession reduced the demand for trucks to a most

*Leyland promotional drawings
showing Roadtrain production.
The cabs are lowered onto the near
complete chassis*

depressing low, for the time being, at least, making the second production line redundant. There was, however, one bright light shining out over Leyland's dark sea of trouble. This was the instant success of T45, the project begun way back in 1974 which had been designed to restore the old dominance of the make on the home trunk routes as well as giving it an at least detectable entry into the fleets of the always very nationalistic European haulage concerns. The first model of the T45 range to appear was a premium artic tractive unit called Roadtrain, a name that seemed to depart completely from Leyland's traditional naming policy which had so often featured the stronger members of the animal world. It has to be admitted that Marathon, Roadtrain's predecessor, was also an odd one out, and Roadtrain is now not alone as its heavy duty sister, coded T43 and intended for export to Third World countries where roads are rare, has been named Landtrain. Roadtrain, especially, can certainly be credited with bringing a new look to the truck world and it was not long after its introduction before it was accorded an honour which acknowledged that it was more than just a pretty face. In competition with the best that Europe could offer, Roadtrain won the 1981 Truck of the Year Award. Commercial vehicle journalists from ten continental countries under the chairmanship of the editor-in-chief of *Truck* magazine voted the new Leyland into first place, thus giving it an accolade worth a very great deal in terms of favourable publicity. So clearly Roadtrain had what it takes to make experienced eyes endorse the real worth of its design and performance characteristics. But everyone concerned knew that from then on success would be measured by the realities of commercial operation where economy and reliability loom very much larger than anything else. Both are to a great extent dependent on the design and build quality of the power plant.

Production prototype testing was extensive. Leyland wanted to make absolutely sure that they had a winner on their hands before it was made available for sale

In view of the dismal reputation gained, maybe justifiably, maybe not, by the post war British automotive industry for the alleged mechanical unreliability of its products, Leyland had very sound reasons for looking long and hard at its existing test procedures. The result was the initiation

of an ambitious scheme for trying to assume the world leadership in the line testing of diesel engines. The plan was to establish a large scale automated engine proving centre and this was finished in good time for every Roadtrain power unit to be quality tested by computer. Cynics with bitter experience of components surviving severe and sophisticated test procedures only to fail immediately when put into service may scoff at the faith shown in computers, but the fact remains that the most conscientious humans cannot compete with computers in the infinitely boring realms of repeatable testing to consistent standards. The diesel test centre was commissioned in 1979 and, since then, engines coming off the production line of the Spurrier works have been transferred to a pre-test rigging area. Here each unit is placed on a carrier trolley which enables all connections for oil, fuel, water and so on., to be made to standard front and rear mounting plates. Transducers are attached and adaptors fitted to the exhaust outlets. The engine is then ready to go off on its travels and runs over a trackway system which eventually brings it to a vacant test cell, one of a total of 64. There the carrier is floated off the track by using compressed air to inflate hover pads attached beneath it. Inside the cell, the engine is bedded down on to anti-vibration mountings, service connections are plugged in and couplings made to a dynamometer and smoke meter.

RIGHT: *Engine sub-assemblies make their way on unmanned trucks to vacant test bed cells. British Leyland have a very modern plant to manufacture their fresh Roadtrain*

BELOW: *This test rig is both large and complicated. Articulated trucks need their trailer attached for comprehensive testing results. A Roadtrain prototype sits on this suspension/chassis rig. Note the weights on the trailer*

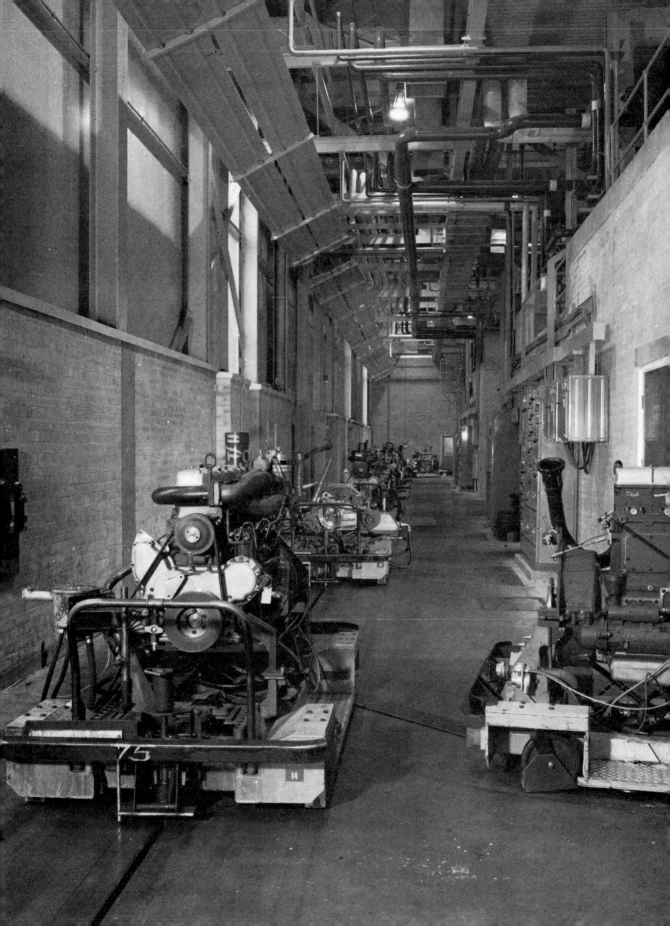

The first step in the test is to crank the engine to make sure it turns over freely. This is done via a local control panel. Then the unit is fired up and the operator transfers from the local control panel to the sound-proofed central console. Each engine has its own plastic identification card which is inserted into a satellite computer. The latter scans the card and selects the appropriate test programme. Once the engine is running, the computer continually scans the sensor read-outs to ensure that no safety parameter is exceeded. If it is (say low oil pressure or high water temperature) the engine is automatically shut down, lights flash and a horn sounds. If the test proceeds with no sign of this sort of trauma developing, the computer runs the engine to achieve certain set values for speed, load, water and oil temperatures. As these are reached, recordings are made of speed, delivered torque, engine pressures and temperatures, fuel delivery and smoke emission. This completed, the computer shuts the throttle and the operator then makes any necessary mid-test adjustments with the crankshaft at idling speed. Finally, the computer cycles the engine through a series of set points and records its performance, compares the test results with the pre-determined specification and only concludes the test when the results are satisfactory.

Neither Roadtrain's powerplant nor any of the other major mechanical components are new and completely untried in service. Totally new in every sense of the word, however, is the C40 cab which itself won an award from the Design Council on T45 launch day. Leyland's brief to the firm given the job of designing the new cab showed much concern for its likely visual impact on a public conditioned by self-appointed protectors of the environment crying 'Juggernaut!'. Ogle Design, the company involved, came up with a shape which was claimed to look much less aggressive than most other comparable cab designs. Certainly, the popular beetle-browed look had gone, so had the pugnacious squared-off grille. The whole effect was one of unobtrusive neatness which is

ABOVE: *The futuristic Leyland accoustic chamber lined entirely with fibreglass wedges. Isolation of individual sound sources is essential in any noise reduction programme*

ABOVE LEFT: *The result of a five year programme, the first in line for the Leyland T45 truck range. This is the Roadtrain 16.28 coupled to a Crane Fruehauf box semi*

presumably what the Leyland management had in mind. Of more tangible importance was the excellent aerodynamic efficiency of the new cab shape as proved by extensive wind tunnel testing. Strictly from the ease of manufacturing angle, the C40 excels because of its modular method of construction which enables any combination of three heights, two widths and three lengths to be built. The number of variations possible actually means that the C40 is a family of cabs, one that could have as many as eighteen members if Leyland is able to find a use for them all. The second son of C40 was a slimmed down model (the narrower of the two possible widths) fitted to another member of the T45 family, a lightweight 32 ton artic tractor christened 'Cruiser'.

With trucks like these now emerging from the Lancashire plant, the road transport scene has to be brightened by the prospect of British designed and built tractive units regaining much of the ground so shamefully lost to imports. Maybe then the humanoid trucks, which surely still run from little boys' homes to school and other more exciting places, will all be Leylands again; or, at least, fewer of them brrm brrming along the paths and pavements will be Scanias, Volvos, Dafs or Mercs.

There should be even better things to come from Europe's most modern truck plant, as this is now backed up by a brand new research centre and test track built by Leyland near Preston and quite close to the very first stretch of motorway to be opened in Britain. Rather like this country with its motorways, Leyland was late in the day in getting its own technical centre. For the time being, of course, the centre will keep Leyland well ahead in the test facilities field. Covering no less than 140 acres, the new complex contains an enormous variety of test equipment, some of it of massive proportions. Biggest of all is a fully isolated concrete room weighing all of 1400 tonnes. It is mounted on springs and lined with hundreds of futuristic-looking fibreglass wedges designed to kill all sounds generated in the chamber. Inside, the air is so dead that all speech has an eerie, flat quality and breathing seems to be something of an unaccustomed effort. Trucks under test in the acoustic chamber get nowhere fast even when driven flat out, as they are mounted on a 400 horse power chassis dynamometer or rolling road. This particular road can roll at speeds up to 80 mph, so noise and vibration measurements can therefore be made with a vehicle which is, in effect, running flat out under a full load, and this under scientifically repeatable conditions. Noise suppression is of growing importance and it is only by using a sophisticated acoustic chamber that individual sounds can be isolated. A major problem with vehicle noise is that a particular type of sound may be more irritable to the ear at low volume than another type at high volume.

Another even more awe-inspiring test rig is set in a seismic block weighing about 1000 tonnes and mounted on air cushions. The latter serve to prevent vibrations induced by a ride simulator, which may be wracking a truck chassis to destruction, from reaching any of the other installations in the building. Anything from a single nut and bolt to a complete artic can be subjected to the treatment. The ultimate durability testing has to be done on the road, but there is no escape from having to accelerate this type of work if development is not to take an unacceptably long time. Yet another chamber which has to be truck-sized is the one in which extreme temperature testing takes place. This is a widely publicised activity of all vehicle manufacturers but obviously the truck maker is faced with providing for the most extreme of extreme conditions. He builds the vehicles that have to keep going when all the rest have stopped. With pressures for better noise suppression increasing, high temperature operation could pose almost insuperable problems. Encapsulation of the power unit may well become necessary to meet future legislative requirements. This should keep the noise in, but it will make getting the heat out that much more difficult.

That part of the research centre which simply has to be of most interest

Designed to minimise driver fatigue; Leyland's T45 interior. Instrument panel is a pinnacle of design excellence

to the admirers of trucks on the move is the test track. Leyland claims that this is not simply a random collection of roads but more a carefully designed instrument over which vehicles can be run to verify the results obtained in the test laboratories. Thus every bump, twist and turn is said to have been designed to serve a specific purpose. The high speed circuit consists of a long, oval loop with bends banked as steeply as 20 degrees through which trucks can be driven 'hands-off' if the driver is brave enough. 'High' speed on the circuit means a maximum of 75 mph, but elsewhere trucks trundle round and round for hour after hour over surfaces which can virtually destroy a chassis at less than half this speed. Within the perimeter track there are hills of varying gradients ranging from 1 in 15 to 1 in 4, smooth straights for brake testing, far from smooth stretches where a thorough job of making fierce corrugations and laying uneven pave has been done, steering pads, water troughs and sprays. A track-side workshop is available for vehicles needing minor attention, an essential time-saver which also avoids disturbing the work of the main workshops where the major modifications required by the various test programmes are carried out. In keeping with the regard for the quality of the environment that every organisation involved in the manufacture and operation of heavy vehicles must now have, Leyland has erected a hefty perimeter fence which screens off from the outside world the noise of the test trucks whether they are circling the speed track or pounding over the pave. Or it may be intended more to screen new models from the prying eyes of competitors! In the old days it would have been said that the local inhabitants preferred hearing the noise from the works which employed so many of them. What they dreaded was despairing silence that meant unemployment.

Dwarfed into insignificance by a veritable host of factories which never seem to have stopped multiplying during the last eighty years or so, Leyland is a little town with a big name known the world over, although, when people with no knowledge of central Lancashire utter it, the last thing they are likely to be thinking of is an untidy cluster of houses and factory buildings hard by the busy M6. But the few streets of red brick houses, interspersed by a line or two of shops and presided over by the blackened stone church, very much belong to the history of road transport in Britain and many other parts of the world. The firm that was quickly to become a giant in their midst had its roots in the village smithy. Like many others of the day, the Leyland blacksmith's shop was developed into a small engineering business during the early part of the 19th century. The business was eventually inherited by one James Sumner, descendant of a long line of blacksmiths but more interested in applying power to transport than in shoeing horses. Sumner actually produced a steam wagon in 1884. It was the first vehicle to be built and operated in Leyland. Like all the early pioneers of powered road transport, he soon found himself hamstrung by restrictive legislation and the object of public hostility. The advent of the Spurrier family into the business brought in more expertise and finance and happened to coincide with the birth of a more favourable legislative climate. As a result, the Lancashire Steam Motor Company was formed in 1896. In 1907, the firm

Landtrain on the rack:
sophisticated electro-hydraulic rigs
can simulate stress caused by the
worst operating conditions

became Leyland Motors Ltd., and the name of the little Lancashire town was well on the way to becoming a household word.

By then, both steam and petrol powered vehicles were being produced, the score turning out to be in favour of steam by a ratio of two to one. The firm was unique in manufacturing both types of prime mover and the production of steamers was not to be phased out until as late as 1926. The success of the Leyland ic engined trucks in the War Office Subsidised Vehicle Trials of 1912 ensured the firm's strong participation in the war effort between 1914 and 1918 when just under 6000 vehicles were produced for the military. At the end of the war many of them were bought back and re-conditioned before being sold for peace-time use. Leyland's founder, James Sumner, retired in 1919 when Henry Spurrier, (known as Henry the Second, his father was Henry the First) became chairman and managing director, a position he was to hold right through to 1963 when ill health forced him to retire. Just before he left, Leyland Motors had become the Leyland Motor Corporation after taking over its biggest rival in the heavy truck business, Associated Commercial Vehicles Ltd., makers of the memorable AEC Mammoths and Mammoth Majors. In the process, the venerable marque names of Maudslay and Thornycroft were acquired. Albion and Scammell were already inside the fold and Guy was to follow soon. The range of products had widened to such an extent, that trucks were no longer paramount in the scheme of things. Rapid expansion had gone on almost without a break for three quarters of a century, but despite the acquisition of manufacturing plants in many part of Britain outside Lancashire as well as in other parts of the world, the headquarters remained where it all began, in the town of Leyland. And it was there, behind the crescent-shaped face of the HQ office block that complacency set in. Export successes continued to be achieved and apparently it was thought that the long-standing domination of the home market was to continue indefinitely. Even the spreading of the motorway network right to the very front door of the birthplace failed to ring the alarm bells. It seems strange that a company with such a vast experience of trading world-wide should have been so unaware of the likely consequences of a lowering of European trade barriers. In 1967 came a reduction in import duties between the member countries of EFTA. The UK was a member, so was Sweden, and in the same year Swedish trucks began to be landed in Britain. There was nothing spectacular about their initial sales performance and there was still time for Leyland to re-shape its model range to enable the sales staff to go out and beat the invaders. worse was to come when finally Britain joined the Common Market, thus throwing open the door to trucks manufactured in the EEC countries.

The Leyland official history records that in 1973 the company entered a new market with the introduction of a maximum capacity truck, the Marathon. This was exactly seven years after the first Scania tractive units designed for 40 ton operation were landed on British soil. The early service history of the Marathon showed well enough that the seven years had not gone in the development of a Swede-beater, the new Leyland materialising as something of a hasty lash-up, destined to do the marque

T43 Landtrain is the Leyland truck with a bonnet. Designed for export, this example tries the test track water splash

Up the 1 in 4 incline at Leyland's test track. Secrecy is important as the high containing fence suggests

more harm than good. Matters were improved a little by the advent of Marathon II which turned out to be a somewhat better effort but, even then, it was none too hot for a second attempt. So it did little to stem the import tide, and foreign trucks were able to go on and maintain their supremacy over the British heavy haulage scene virtually unchallenged.

The T45 story admits that the Marathon was an interim truck, as it tells how the project was well under way long before the company's first top weight tractor came on the market. It may have been better for the Leyland reputation if Marathon had never been born, though the fact remains that things had been allowed to get to the stage where any decision was likely to be the wrong one. The T45 story so far indicates that the next decision was a correct one. It was decided to plan for the eighties by starting with a clean sheet of paper and pulling out every possible stop in a carefully calculated attempt to design and build a top weight truck that could really beat the pants off the opposition. The engineers concerned were quick to realise that they were being given the chance of a lifetime. They knew that none of them would ever again get the opportunity to participate in such a project, as brand new truck designs in the future are not going to be called for more than once a generation. They were well aware of the fact that though the final product was unlikely to be a masterpiece of highly advanced technology, every possible technological aid had to be brought in to assist with its designing, development and ultimate manufacture. Hence the reason for the parallel planning of an advanced engineering test facility and an ultra-sophisticated assembly plant.

Reports of the early days of the T45 project suggest that the first sheet of drawing paper was so clean that it was obvious that no decision on whether the new vehicle would be a conventional design, or a revolutionary one, had been taken, or was to be taken until things were well under way. Nevertheless, it does seem unlikely that anything other than the normal layout using a front-mounted engine beneath the floor of a rectangular forward control cab was ever seriously considered; especially as an initial assessment of the most important needs of the transport operator concluded that a revolutionary transport machine had little attraction for its user. In the light of this finding, it was perfectly predictable that the new design would turn out to be evolutionary rather than revolutionary. Inevitably, many of those involved in the complex and imprecise process of attempting to predict market trends, of trying to decide what sort of earning performance would be demanded of trucks halfway into the eighties and beyond, must still have been guided mainly by the gut feeling telling them that what was really needed was a design which would earn the lasting loyalty of the drivers by cossetting them in their cabs, as well as the gratitude of the operators by being more frugal of fuel and downtime than any of the opposition. If this was so, it explains why one of the first moves was the logical and practical step of putting the best and newest competitive European trucks under the microscope. Altogether, over forty special reports were commissioned, twenty two of them concerning the driver and his cab. In the end, of course, the T45 emerged as a completely conventional design using components which in

Leyland's Scammell Constructor is another model in the Roadtrain range. Eight wheeler bulk tanker is unquestionably handsome

the main had been tried and tested in other applications. It would be quite wrong to assume from this that Leyland were simply serving up the mixture as before. If bits from the Marathon were going to be used, the fact that they had apparently worked well in that application was not to be accepted at face value. They still had to prove themselves in exhaustive testing, and, if modified for any reason, to prove themselves again.

It was firmly decided that this time all the development would be done by the manufacturer, nothing of this was to be laid at the door of the customer as had tended to happen too frequently in the past. New targets for performance and durability were often set, as occurred with the braking system which was required to provide double the normally accepted lining life with improved retardation and less routine attention. Securing the largest possible lining area within a given drum size dictated the use of twin wedge shoe expanders as in the Girling Twinstop system. But even after the Leyland engineers decided to go for this, it took four years of testing and modification before they were satisfied that the required targets could be reached. The unprecedented (for Leyland) volume of component testing required the prolonged use of many laboratory rigs and a fleet of more than 80 test vehicles (not T45 prototypes) which, over a period of five years, covered a total of about four million miles. Testing in actual service was regarded as the final arbiter of a component's reliability and durability, and Leyland town is a good place to start from if a punishing road circuit is the prime requirement. The backbone of England, the rugged Pennines, rear up to the east of the M6, and the test trucks had not far to go to encounter steep, serpentine gradients linked by cambered, narrow roads with poor surfaces. These northern hills are also crossed by motorways that soar and swoop across the undulating moors, so it is far from difficult to take in roads that make trucks have to contend with a mixture of running conditions that vary almost from minute to minute. This extremely arduous mile-eating had to go on day and night, summer and winter. Other test trucks had things even harder climatically, being sent to winter in the snows of northern Canada. Time was always the enemy, there is no way of amassing such mammoth mileages quickly, and the building of the actual prototypes could not wait until all component testing was completed. Prototype building did, however, proceed only slowly, mainly because they were intended to emerge eventually as vehicles which could be put together on the assembly line, not as one-off, hand-made specials. Prototype testing was to add another one and a half million to the total of test miles.

With the prototypes tried, tested and proved, there was yet one more stage to go through before assembly could begin on the new lines. It was intended to produce about two hundred pre-production T45s and to do this a pilot production line was set up in a part of the existing truck plant. Here the validity of the proposed build procedure was thoroughly tested and it says a great deal for the long term efforts of the planning teams that necessary modifications to the assembly programme were few, amounting merely to some changes in the order of offering certain components to the chassis.

Some of these pre-production models went into service with the Leyland test fleet, the others were sent out into the cold, unsympathetic world of commercial operation to serve as guinea pigs under the scrutiny of selected transport fleet managers, and, of course, at the hands of their drivers. So the T45s finally met the men whose opinions really mattered. Leyland acknowledged that there could be a world of difference between the naturally sympathetic handling of the company's test drivers and the demanding approach of the professional driver concerned only with getting his load safely from A to B in the minimum of time. The engineering team, which had taken fully five years to progress from clean sheet of paper to finished truck, could now only hope and pray that all their work had been good enough. They were able to breathe a little easier when the first feedbacks from the fleets sounded no alarm bells, and took additional comfort from the satisfyingly smooth progress of the first production trucks along the all-new assembly line, proof enough of the value of the carefully thought-through pre-production programme.

It is easy now for an outsider to claim that the new 14 acre plant began turning out trucks just about twelve months too late. By the time the T45s were streaming freely out through the giant exit doors, recession had cut the demand from an all-time high to a near disastrous low. The two highly automated lines have a double shift capacity of over 400 truck and bus chassis per week, far beyond anything that could be expected in the way of customer demand during 1980 and 1981, or even 1982. As matters stand at present, the forecasting of the likely demand for T45 seems to have been the one thing that went sadly wrong.

But even when operating at only part capacity, with components that should be in the racks of the vast, fully automated warehouse, stored beneath the conveyors of the idle line, the new assembly hall is an impressive place. Its very immensity as a single building inspires an immediate sense of awe. To walk its length and breadth is to foot it for as far as half a kilometre, a jogger would notch up the miles pretty quickly by running from end to end, with only two round trips needed to register each mile. Though the making of a truck involves a tremendous number of processes, the final coming together of the multitude of small and large components is the phase that generates the most interest and excitement. This is especially true of the most automated plants, the activities of robots apparently fascinating more than the working of mere men. The Leyland design team was able to study closely how the rest of the world tackled truck assembly and in the end to claim that they had built the world's most advanced facility. Fortunately, when the planners had done their job, the money was there to convert their plans into reality.

And the reality of the most modern truck plant is that machines cannot take over to the extent they have elsewhere, the men still build the trucks, the machines supply the muscle and a computer sees that the parts are in the right place at the right time. Its programme has to cater for a random mix of all the projected models in the T45 truck family plus the underfloor engined chassis of the Leopard coach. They are all born on a moving floor conveyor where the chassis frames take shape as the various members are bolted together. A locking chemical is used to prevent any loosening of the fastenings in service whilst allowing them to be undone if repairs become necessary. All the chassis begin life upside down to make attachment of suspension and axles simpler. With these attached, the still wheel-less chassis are turned the right way up and then hung from an overhead conveyor that loops its way across and along the breadth and length of the hall. Growth goes on steadily as engine, gearbox, radiator, fuel tank and wiring are added, then the whole chassis is covered with two coats of paint, a bright-looking silver finish for export models, a very funeral black for the home market vehicles. This, rather surprisingly, is how the respective customers like it. Emergence from the spray booth is followed by the lubricating of all chassis bearings, then the wheels go on. Still cabless, and hence looking strangely insignificant in such surroundings, the now rolling chassis finds its wheels but has to only creep along on the back of another moving floor conveyor. Meanwhile, the cab specifically intended for it has been progressing along a paint line under the same, vast roof. The cabs are finished in any one of six colours, then pass to the trim line where the colour coordinated interior takes shape and seats, wiring and instruments are installed. Then comes the moment of mating chassis and cab, and, quite suddenly it seems, another Roadtrain, Cruiser or Constructor assumes its characteristic face and is almost ready to become one of the world's workers. But first it has to prove its potential on the rollers of one of the three dynamometers that lie between it and the world outside. Once off the rolling road after putting up a satisfactory performance, the new truck goes off to meet its owner, or less happily but more likely in the current economic climate, to take its place on the stocking ground.

14 What is it?

Necessary evil . . . far horizons . . . along the Interstates . . . on-going source . . . state of flux . . . detective ability . . . big badge . . . baffled by paint . . . Rolls legend . . . from the animals . . . never dull . . . care needed! . . . nervous of cameras . . . easier on approaches . . . filling the frame . . . distorts proportions . . . danger involved!

Seddon Atkinson. Easy to spot. Many of them have the traditional Atkinson 'A'

To the uninitiated, the heavy truck presents something of a hostile and frightening image by appearing to be, at worst, an alien, mis-used machine that is doing a job more appropriate to the freight train, at best a noisy, somewhat dangerous though useful monster which can be reluctantly accepted only as a necessary evil. The road transport industry itself is probably more on the defensive than it need be, tending to regard the obvious hatred of the more extreme environmentalists as being more representative of the ordinary individual views than it really is. Much of

the anti-truck lobby is made up of the protagonists of transport modes which still exist only by virtue of vast injections of public money. As the Armitage Committee has pointed out, the elevation of the truck to its dominance in the economy was accomplished by the customers, and virtually everyone in the land has chosen to be a customer of one or more of the firms which make up the direct customers of road transport.

Daf tells you more than most manufacturers: 2800 Turbo Intercooling, or is that just advertising?

Those people who look beyond the jaundiced and biassed opinions of the avowed enemies of road transport are likely to find the current trucking scene of absorbing interest. The modern long distance truck itself has become a most impressive, sophisticated vehicle disposing of the sort of power which can otherwise be commanded on the road only by the drivers of gas guzzling super cars. The modern trucker himself has all this power at his toes and finger tips. His everyday horizons lie far beyond those of the majority of people doing jobs of supposedly far greater status and apparently offering far more in the way of opportunity. He regularly covers ground that represents for the more ambitious holiday motorist a promised land accessible only once a year at great expense for no more than a paltry week or so. The truck enthusiast can let his admiration loose on either man or machine, or both, in the sure knowledge that it can be exercised almost everywhere he is likely to go by road and at virtually any hour of the day or night.

Unlike the rail buff, who is faced with continually shrinking activity or, in many areas, a complete cessation of all movement, the truck lover looks in on a scene that has the vitality of an operation no modern nation can do without. Whether he is near or far from his home he regularly encounters the objects of his admiration and very often a feast can become a surfeit during any journey that embraces a trunk route or motorway, and a movable feast can be transformed into a static one by visiting a busy service area. On regular view will be a wide variety of makes and models originating from many countries, almost all of them artics with semi-trailers of various types carrying an enormous spread of types of cargo. There is always the chance of spotting a rare bird with origins remote from Europe, a Mack, or a White or a giant Kenworth looking as if it would be more at home hammering along the US Interstates; or perhaps a Hino made in Japan though assembled just across the Irish Sea, or, more rarely, a truck with a strange-sounding name that could only have been built behind the Iron Curtain. Trucks with unusual number plates are not really uncommon and many of them are obviously up to a couple of thousand miles away from base.

The Ford Transcontinental (this one is Spanish registered) has a very tall cab which is difficult to mistake

However, to make the most of the truck spotting hobby a certain amount of self-education is necessary. This can be an easy and pleasurable process as the trucking scene is covered amply and expertly by a number of periodicals. Understandably, some of these are aimed mainly at the operators of freight and passenger carrying vehicles, though all of them do include a great deal of information of interest to the enthusiast. But probably the best on-going source of information for the dedicated truck buff is a monthly magazine called simply: *Truck*. This sets out to feature in a big way all the stars of the trunk routes and motorways by publishing very comprehensive road tests designed to interest and inform operators,

Renault, Saviem, Berliet . . . and Ford share the same basic cab. Look beyond the sun visor and compare the Renault with the Spanish Transconti on page 161

drivers and outside enthusiasts. Although there is a natural concentration on European topics, the global scene is not forgotten, and world wide coverage is given to all the technical, political and economic aspects of truck building and operation.

Initially the task of absorbing detailed information about the vast range of makes and models with their seemingly endless span of engine and transmission permutations appears to be more than a little daunting. There is no denying the fact that the trucking world is in a fairly constant state of flux and it is necessary to establish some sort of a base line from which to work at the process of keeping up to date. If this book is to achieve its intended purpose, the reader should find that by the time he/she reaches the end, sufficient information on who makes what will have been gleaned to enable an intelligible picture to be built up.

Depending on how you look at it, the various makers' apparent reluctance to use any sort of easily understood system of designating their various wares can make truck spotting more or less interesting. Nevertheless, anyone with any pretensions to even slight detective ability will undoubtedly enjoy looking for the clues that certainly do exist. No such reticence is shown in informing the world of the actual make of a particular truck. This is done in giant letters in the most prominent place by Leyland, Scania, Volvo, Daf, Man, Foden, ERF, Bedford and Renault. Seddon Atkinson, Magirus Deutz and Fiat use rather less explicit though still easily readable lettering, whilst Ford rely on the oval, blue badge which is universally applied to all their vehicles from Fiesta to Transcontinental, making only the obvious concession of giving the trucks a bigger badge than the cars. One European maker relies solely on a badge, admittedly a big one and probably the one best known and revered in the automotive world. The Mercedes-Benz three pointed star is, of course, also used on the prestigious cars made by the German firm of Daimler-Benz. On the trucks it is giant sized and displayed without any accompanying lettering. The rather similar big 'A' (for Atkinson) has reappeared on some Seddon Atkinsons but the SA grille bears no relationship to the one used by Mercedes. Also very easy to recognise is another German truck, the Man. Its sharply rectangular and narrowish front grille shows up well even when a relatively long way off. Current car grille fashions have been adopted by several makers, notably Scania, Fiat and Magirus Deutz with their full width patterns. Some rarely seen makes are also easily identifiable, like the American Mack with its name just as prominently displayed as any other. Another American design, the White, may sometimes appear to be quite anonymous yet possesses an outline which becomes quite distinctive on close acquaintance, partly because of the far forward position of the front axle. Other US trucks have the same characteristic.

A truck profile is, of course, governed mainly by the shape of its cab. It is quite true that at first sight one truck cab looks virtually identical to another, but when the differences begin to be appreciated it becomes difficult to believe that it was ever possible to confuse one with another. In most instances the differences, initially seeming rather subtle, turn out

BELOW: *This one's a TR280 Turbo Renault*

*Magirus Deutz 256M19FS 40
tonner built under the IVECO
agreement. Deutz engine is an air-
cooled V8 of 12.76 litres*

to be quite substantial, remarkably so in view of the unity of purpose all the designers must share. The subtleties have to be worked pretty hard when more than one make uses the same basic cab design, something far from being unknown in an industry where a particular make can be little more than a specific combination of bought-in components. Sometimes, the most experienced spotter can be baffled temporarily by an operator's own paint job which effectively changes the outline of the grille, and sometimes of the whole cab. This seems to happen quite a lot to Scanias, maybe because the unadorned front of the Swedish cab tends to be somewhat featureless. Leyland Roadtrains and Cruisers also seem to be especially prone to this sort of camouflage. Some owners actually remove the manufacturer's name, others change it for their own, sometimes by quite crafty means, one example being the transformation of Leyland into Redland by two easy letter substitutions, in effect turning a truck into a tile!

But in any case, identification from the side or from points to the side and rear is essentially a matter of recognising the cab shape, although wheels can be a recognition feature especially when they are of cast and not pressed manufacture, a fact that almost certainly proves that the truck is of continental origin. The arrangement of the cab side windows is a useful pointer, so is that of the rear windows if any are present. Fuel tank position and shape provides further evidence, as does the disposition of the air reservoirs and cab steps. Having once established the make of a particular truck, it is then very satisfying to be able to deduce something of its mechanical specification. As already mentioned, the clues to this vary very much from one make to another. Some of them are provided by the engine builders, Rolls-Royce being notable in this respect. Often, though, the RR plaque attached to the front panel tells no more than the fact that an Eagle diesel is under the bonnet, or, rather, under the cab. Bigger, more explanatory plaques can be seen, however, such as the Rolls one bearing the legend 265L, showing that the resident Eagle is a 12 litre turbocharged, low speed economy tuned unit developing 265 bhp. Much rarer and seldom as informative are badges indicating that a Gardner or a Cummins unit is the prime mover.

The manufacturers who fit their own engines exclusively usually manage to convey a certain amount of information via the grille badge. A DAF displaying a model number such as 2300 probably has 230 bhp available though this is not certain because it could have a lower power option. No explanation is required when the Dutch firm elaborates by adding words like 'turbo' and 'intercooler'. The leader of the original Swedish truck invasion, Scania, believes in letting the customer choose the make of power unit he wants providing it is a Scania, and if it comes with, say the legend 112 m inscribed below the grille he knows it will have an 11 litre engine installed in a chassis designed for medium duty. Choosing one of the biggest of the Scania units will get him a V8 badge on the front. The other Swede, so beloved of many of the long haul drivers, Volvo, usually carries its model number on a badge placed centrally on the grille, the number itself indicating how many litres are displaced by the pistons, thus an F10 has a 10 litre capacity and the 'turbo 6' tacked on below elaborates. Notable exceptions to this rule are the F86 and F88 which may or may not display the model number on the cab sides.

Leyland have a long-standing tradition of endowing their trucks with suitable names. The main source of these has been the animal kingdom but there has never been a slavish adherence to this naming policy. After the Marathon, until recently Leyland's flagship, has come the Roadtrain, followed by the Cruiser which took over from the Buffalo and the Lynx. Normally these names are displayed on the nearside front of the cab but, in any case, the C40 cab used on the T45 series is like that of no other Leyland, or of any other truck, for that matter, so instant recognition should be the rule here. Rather more obscure is the meaning of the numbers set on the side of the cab. Four digits in two sets of two make up combinations like 16.28, 16.21 and so on, the first pair indicating the maximum gross weight of the tractor, the second pair the bhp available after a nought has been added. The Roadtrain 16.28 tractor therefore weights 16 tons when fully loaded and 280 bhp is on tap to move it. Keeping tabs on development can bring the reward of not-so-obvious clues. Thus, it can be assumed that a 'V' registered Roadtrain will have a Leyland TL 12 litre powerplant, the 'T' showing that it is turbocharged. The Rolls-Royce and Cummins alternatives were not available until 'W' became the registration suffix.

Mercedes-Benz stick to numbers only and use the same system as Leyland, and were in fact using it first. The Ford Transcontinental range is typed by combining the gross train weight with the available bhp, the

1978 ERF cabover. Typical British truck with 'standard' cab

latter divided by ten, thus 4427 indicates that 270 horsepower is available to propel a maximum gross combination weight of 44 tonnes. The model number may or may not be on display on the cab sides.

As long as the roads are populated by such a wide variety of makes and models, truck spotting can never be dull. When sufficient knowledge has been accumulated to make instant identification fairly easy, counts of passing vehicles can produce some very interesting information. Its collection can be as hectic or as leisurely an activity as the spotter cares to make it. On a busy trunk route, the flow of trucks may be great enough to overwhelm all efforts at keeping an accurate tally. Under such conditions, heavy vehicles have a disturbing habit of arriving in bunches of two or more and it may be possible to get down only the names of the various makes as they pass, and those just from one direction. Where traffic is lighter, there will be time enough to allow the noting of other details as well as keeping track of trucks approaching from both directions. The ultimate in leisurely spotting can be done on the motorway service area truck parks where close examination facilitates accurate identification. However, spotting activities here have to be carried out with some discretion. Drivers should not have to be plagued by spotters wandering carelessly around and between parked vehicles, so venturing on to the tarmac should be undertaken only with the utmost care.

A logical extension of the pastime of simply observing interesting trucks is the production of a photographic record which can later be studied at leisure. Understandably, however, the average driver tends to be nervous of camera toting onlookers, particularly if the equipment used has any sort of professional look about it. After all, he spends his working life under the constant surveillance of the police and knows that at any given moment he could be committing technical offences he is unaware of. So anything that looks like a possible additional check on his activities or whereabouts is bound to make him wonder, even if he knows full well he has nothing to worry about. So the wise and considerate enthusiast asks the driver for permission to shoot before pressing the shutter or even aiming the camera. This, of course, is possible only when the truck in question is parked with the driver in attendance. If he is absent and sees nothing of the camera work there can be no harm done, so shoot away. Photographing trucks on the move is a totally different affair. Drivers spotting the camera cannot guess for sure that trucks are being singled out from other traffic, so are unlikely to think twice about it.

No very sophisticated techniques or equipment are necessary to produce satisfying shots of trucks at work. Probably the best combination of film and camera consists of 35 mm colour reversal film loaded into one of the many and varied single lens reflex models, in fact the sort of equipment that people use to make a record of their holidays. Producing the resulting pictures as colour slides is the most economical method of enabling the subjects to be blown up to a considerable size and viewed on a screen. Film and lens speeds are not in any way critical when shooting in the truck park, but both have to be considered carefully before attempting to get pictures of traffic speeding along a motorway. In these circumstances the faster the film the better if sharp transparencies of

trucks travelling at 60 plus mph are to be obtained. It is, in fact, much easier to get good pictures where trucks are turning into or out of motorway approach roads, there speeds are low and the photographer can get close enough to fill his frame even when using only a standard focus lens.

ABOVE: *Volvo heavy heavyweight. This company has retained its individuality over recent years very well. Left hand drive aids driving this slow, large low loader*

From the more distant vantage points such as a motorway bridge, the subject size will not be satisfactory unless a long focus lens is used. This need not be one of the cumbersome telephoto models so beloved of motor racing enthusiasts and which really need to be set up on a stout tripod if any sort of reasonable result is to be achieved. In general the truck buff should be able to get results he wants by using a medium focus lens of about 150 mm focal length. Both the relatively modest size and weight of such a lens is not enough to make the camera cumbersome or too heavy to be hand held for longish periods without picture-destroying shake developing. And there should be little difficulty in filling the frame if the vantage point is well chosen. In addition, the effective range of a lens of this size can be doubled by fitting one of the converter lenses currently available at a fraction of the cost of a longer focus camera lens. A 2x converter extends the focal length in question to 300 mm and adds virtually nothing to the bulk and weight of the equipment. The main drawback to this set-up is a necessary lengthening of the exposure time, so good results can normally be obtained only when the available light is good and a fast film is used. The lighting problem is, of course, made more acute when fast shutter speeds are necessary. If the camera is held stationary when shooting a truck travelling at 60 or 70 mph, the shutter should be set at 1/500 or 1/1000 of a second. But much slower speeds can be satisfactory providing the camera is panned so as to follow the fast-moving subject. This is a very useful ploy which is well worth practising beforehand though it is easy enough to master quite quickly. Done properly it produces the impressive effect of a sharply defined truck imposed on a blurred background.

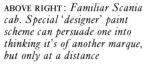

ABOVE RIGHT: *Familiar Scania cab. Special 'designer' paint scheme can persuade one into thinking it's of another marque, but only at a distance*

Of even more value than a fixed lens of about 150 mm focal length is a zoom lens with a range of approximately 35 to 105 mm, again used in conjunction with a 2X converter. The ability to zoom the picture towards or away from the subject is of enormous value when attempting to shoot trucks from varying distances and angles. Filling the frame then becomes very much easier. If dramatic effects are required rather than simple record shots, the wide angle end of the zoom range (35 mm) can be use to distort a truck's proportions, the main effect being to exaggerate its overall length. Another way of giving the subject more impact is to keep the camera close to the ground when shooting.

If prints rather than transparencies are required, the need to fill the frame is not so acute. The camera will then have to be loaded with negative film, either colour or monochrome, and during the ensuing enlargement stage a too small image on the negative can be blown up to fill the finished picture. At the same time errors in exposure time can be corrected. The only trouble with producing large prints is that they are very expensive, On the other hand, a simpler, hence cheaper, camera can be used.

Like the simple observer, the truck photographer can never allow himself to forget that there is danger involved unless sensible precautions are taken. Wandering absent-mindedly across the tarmac of a truck park on a busy service area, thinking more about the last or the next shot than of getting out of the way of moving vehicles, is stupid and hardly fair on the drivers. So is standing on the edge or too close to the edge of any carriageway carrying fast-moving traffic. Remember that one of the senses most relied on to warn of impending danger, that of hearing, tends to be negatived where the level of background noise is high, so the eyes have to do double duty and should never be allowed to drop their guard. Positions occupied on bridges over a motorway should never be above any of the traffic lanes. Dropping something even as small and light as a pencil could form a hazard for a driver passing below.

15 Where to see them?

Automatic blame . . . factories in odd places . . . maintaining the fabric . . . an ill wind . . . exit A5 . . . surprising togetherness . . . spectacular . . . more spectacular . . . traditional link . . . never stops . . . fabulous view . . . evocative sights . . . worthwhile excursion . . . non-motorway . . . a long time coming . . . needless cost.

Modern Europe. Crossing the Alps by tunnel is a modern phenomena which has made road transport quicker and therefore more efficient. Dazzled Daf 2800 sees the light of day once again.

Truck operators and their drivers are the people who seem to get most of the blame for the more undesirable aspects of the impact of road transport on the environment. Putting aside the fact that the far greater numbers of lesser vehicles are often more responsible for these than the truck, the plain truth is that industrialists, politicians and trade unions, both past and present, are much more blameworthy. The road transport industry is far from being responsible for the industrial geography of Britain. Logically enough, the founders of the industrial revolution established their factories where the relevant raw materials happened to be. Thus great conurbations like the one centred on Birmingham and the West Midlands grew up far away from the ports through which its people had to be fed and the merchandise they produced could be exported. Since then, successive generations of industrial planners have planted factories in all sorts of odd places, often without regard for the non-existence of vital transport links. The versatility of the truck saved many such projects from instant disaster and it still goes on helping to maintain the fabric of a society which the politicians proudly proclaim to be one of 'choice'. Purely in transport terms, this means that every truck carrying, say, 20 tons of Brand X merchandise from London to Manchester (or anywhere else) will inevitably pass another truck carrying 20 tons of Brand Y identical merchandise from Manchester to London. Moreover, the odds are that when they pass each other on their respective return journeys, both trucks will be running empty.

To order things differently seems to be beyond the wit of current industrial man, maybe because the necessary powers are possessed only by the leaders of totalitarian states and these are far from being a good advertisement for their particular methods of promoting efficiency. However, it is an ill wind, and the obvious beneficiary of the present apparently chaotic and uneconomic system is no other than the truck enthusiast! He has only to look at an up to date motorway map to find out where he can feast his eyes on a never-ending procession of the machines he so admires. Making the transport system more efficient would undoubtedly cut the number of trucks on view, good for the environment, perhaps, but definitely somewhat frustrating for the keen truck spotter.

171

ABOVE: *Overcrowding even on motorways is a problem which needs an urgent solution. Leyland Marathon cab looks very dated now*

LEFT: *Part loads are inefficient although sometimes inevitable. Tilt trailers of this sort ease loading and unloading. This 40 foot trailer pulled by a Volvo is obviously of European origin*

Since 1960 when the M1 was opened and the old A5 fell into relative disuse, most trucks leaving London for the industrial West Midlands have taken the motorway route. The subsequent extension of M1 to Leeds and the opening of M6 to the north west as far as Carlisle soon brought in trucks bound to and from these parts, so there is always plenty to see en route and on the service areas. Scratchwood SA is only half a dozen miles from where M1 begins at its junction with the notoriously congested North Circular Road, and it is not surprising that south-bound vehicles tend to predominate on the extensive truck park. The Scratchwood site is all on the north-bound side of the carriageways, an overbridge bringing in south-bound traffic. Toddington Services comes up next, soon after the old A5 is crossed close to one of the old truck stops that still survives in the shadow of the motorway. The Toddington truck park slopes awkwardly and is somewhat cramped, but only a dozen miles on the Newport Pagnell SA is laid out on more generous lines with ample truck parking and a covered bridge to link the two sides. Next comes the almost new Rothersthorpe Services, much less cramped than the old-established Watford Gap site. Taking the M6 branch at Junction 19, Corley SA comes up next, usually well-populated with trucks and much more spacious than the one at Hilton Park, on the far edge of the Midlands conurbation. It was here that three Macks were spotted in surprising togetherness, one French, one Spanish and one British registered.

Further north still, Keele SA offers only limited parking for trucks, but then comes Sandbach with plenty of space, perhaps in deference to the local truck makers, Foden and ERF. Charnock Richard, just short of the truck town of Leyland, is again somewhat cramped for big vehicles. Likewise, Forton SA, just to the south of Lancaster, has only a smallish truck park and the one-sided (southbound) Killington Lane and (northbound) Tebay areas offer the trucker even less elbow room. But Southwaite SA, not far from where the M6 ends just to the north of Carlisle, is quite generously endowed and a fruitful place for keen spotters.

The Tebay to Penrith section of the M6 is one of the most spectacular stretches of motorway in Britain. Junction 39 happens to coincide with Shap Summit and here the surrounding open moorland makes for the easy observing of a normally constant procession of big trucks operating in a most impressive setting. A drive to the highest point of the old route followed by the A6 is unlikely to yield much in the way of interesting heavy vehicles, but it will show what the truckers of not so long ago had to contend with. Only a little imagination is needed to conjure up a convincing picture of the chaos extreme weather conditions could induce.

Even more spectacular are the highest sections of the M62, the trans-Pennine motorway which has revolutionized travel between Lancashire and Yorkshire. The M62 has a good claim to being as breathtaking as any comparable highway in the world, especially when seen from the fine viewpoint where the A6025 crosses it. There is never any shortage of trucks to see, and on some stretches, where the M62 tends to be more

steeply graded than its counterparts elsewhere in Britain, even the more powerful tractive units have to work hard to keep up the momentum on the long, sustained climbs. Both the Birch and Hartshead SAs have plenty of parking space for trucks, as they should have on a motorway that seems to carry as many heavies each day as the busiest parts of the network.

Not all the great trunk roads of the pre-motorway era lost importance as the new road system spread its tentacles more and more widely. Perhaps the most celebrated of all Britain's highways was the old Great North Road, classified as the A1 and the traditional link between London and Edinburgh. Now the A1 is an all dual carriageway route as far as the conurbation of Tyneside. It incorporates some longish lengths of motorway and its northern half, particularly, fairly teems with trucks, despite the 40 mph speed limit which applies where it serves as an all-purpose road, and is especially irritating for the long haul men. A1 still goes all the way to Edinburgh but is reduced to a single carriageway long before the Scottish border is reached, so truckers have a much easier way to Scotland in the shape of the M6. Maybe the Great North Road is no longer 'great' by comparison with the major motorways. It does, however, form a busy feeder route for the east coast ferry ports and is a very worthwhile hunting ground for the enthusiast bored with the sameness of the motorways. For many truckers, it scores by still having a number of popular truck stops which they can regard as their own domain, unlike the motorway service areas that have to be shared with the general ruck of road users.

The routes to the ports are naturally where the greatest concentrations of international traffic can be seen. From the spotter's point of view, the

Going North. The standard work from this ERF on the Great North Road; not a motorway but a now acceptable main trunk road. These roads now tend to be clear of trucks

Over the top of the Dover Harbour Board's Eastern Dock goes the new bypass, typical of the very necessary roadwork now being completed throughout Britain. This 40 foot Berliet would have caused havoc in Dover's town

fact that this traffic never stops makes these routes all the more interesting. Inland truck traffic does, of course, slacken off during week ends and some readers might imagine that spotting can only be a strictly weekday activity, and a normal working hours weekday at that. However, this is far from being the case. Trucks do not simply evaporate on the stroke of 1700 hours. The flow of short haul vehicles obviously slackens towards the end of the ordinary worker's day, but long distance haulage is far from being ordinary work. A week-end trip along the A2/M2 route to the busy Kent port of Dover can demonstrate how true this is. In rather typical fashion, truckers then get a pretty raw deal by having the only service area, Farthing Corner, swamped by coach trippers whose sheer numbers ensure that squalor usually rules.

So the sensible spotter, like the once bitten trucker, does not linger at Farthing Corner. Fortunately, there are much better things to come when he reaches Dover. At the majority of ports the dock areas tend to be well screened and are inaccessible to curious observers. Thanks, however, to the proximity of the celebrated white cliffs, an utterly fabulous view of the whole operation of the port can be enjoyed. It is possible to climb the cliffs behind the Eastern Docks either by car or on foot to reach vantage points high enough to reveal pretty well everything that goes on, and low enough to be not so remote that ships and vehicles seem like mere toys. There is always a remarkable number of complete artics and unattached semi-trailers to be seen. Ferries arrive and depart at frequent intervals so there is never any shortage of shunting, embarkation and disembarkation movements to watch. Trucks arrive and depart in fairly spectacular fashion through a cleft in the chalk cliffs connected to the docks by a road built on concrete stilts.

Most of the trucks heading for Southampton from London leave the capital via the A4 and M3. The latter carves its way through the Surrey suburbs and on into Hampshire where its only service area lies just across the border. Set in the heart of a pinewood, the truck parks on the Fleet SA see a good variety of interesting vehicles. The London-bound side appears to be more used by continental rigs, and evocative sights like three Spanish tri-axled, twelve wheeled reefers hauled by Pegaso tractors are not unknown. On the final stretch to Southampton, via the A33, London traffic is joined by trucks outward bound from the midlands on the A34. From Winchester to the port is then as busy as any intensive trucking route in the country. Most of the traffic reaches the docks via the M27 and the M271, but some goes on across the open green acres of the New Forest to the freight-only ferry run by Truckline from Poole.

The nearest motorway service area to central London is at Heston on the M4, a location where truck spotting can be combined with plane spotting, thanks to the close vicinity of London Airport. Bristol, with associated Avonmouth, and the industrial belt of South Wales, are the main destinations served by this road. Service areas crop up fairly frequently, most of them quite small though apparently not as overburdened with heavies as those on some of the other motorways. Trucks bound for South Wales can pull off on to the Aust SA just east of the Severn Bridge. This can be a fruitful spot for the spotter as it makes an excellent vantage point from which to watch traffic crossing the bridge. Trucks can also be closely observed when they stop at the toll booths. These are reached by a footpath which eventually leads across the bridge, a worthwhile excursion if the weather is fine.

Of the major motorways, the M5 carries the smallest proportion of truck traffic. Together with the M50 spur and its dual carriageway extension to the M4, it does form an important route from the Birmingham area to South Wales. It is, of course, the main link between the industries of Bristol and Birmingham, and, via the M6, the north west. Beyond Bristol, however, it is a mainly tourist route with a sprinkling of TIR vehicles which use the ro-ro services from Plymouth to the continent.

The A1 has already been mentioned as a mainly non-motorway route always thickly populated with heavies. Comparable in this respect are a few other all-purpose roads, notably the A38 from Birmingham to Derby, Nottingham and the M1, the A74 taking M6 trucks up to Glasgow, the A12 from London to the ferries at Felixstowe and Harwich, and the link from these ports to the industrial Midlands, nominally the A45. This is now a reasonable road as far inland as Cambridge, but it is an ingenious or infinitely patient trucker who can get any further west without becoming thoroughly frustrated. Vital to the Midlands-east coast route is the proposed M1-A1 link, but this is going to be a long time coming just like the scandalously delayed M25 outer ring road for London. Meanwhile, lives will be needlessly lost, transport costs remain needlessly high. As always, the trucker will have to shoulder most of the blame for conditions caused by the short-sightedness of politicians and the arrogant delaying tactics of the environmentalists.

16 Epilogue

Transport face changed . . . determines the spec . . . patient omnipotence . . . similar mix . . . drawbars predominate . . . viable replacement?

The 1949 International Road Transport Union conference in Geneva came up with the idea of covering Europe with a 26,000 mile network of standard pattern roads. This was tied in with a scheme for standardising the construction and use regulations so as to achieve some sort of unity of design in the vehicles intended to run on the new roads. Since then the transport face of Europe has certainly changed, but neither the roads nor the vehicles have been made to conform with standards that know no frontiers. Nevertheless, it is probably true to say that there is less disagreement between the European nations in the sphere of roads and road vehicles than in any other.

Expanding still, though at a decreasing pace, the vast network of motorways has been constructed with a uniformity that facilitates the flow of international traffic across national borders without posing serious problems for vehicles or their drivers. There are, however, some quite glaring gaps in the system which militate against the use of vehicles designed to operate on motorways exclusively. The idea of boring road tunnels through the great Alpine barrier that cuts Italy off from the rest of Europe came with the original scheme for the standardisation of the road system. Specifically mentioned then was the Mont Blanc tunnel, a project which has long been completed yet is still cut off from the motorway systems of both France and Italy. So trucks can reach the tunnel entrances only after long, hard climbs over narrow and twisting roads, these very often being clogged with tourist traffic. Those relatively few uncharacteristic kilometres in effect determine the specification of a truck designed to operate, say, between Paris and Rome, and it will be so until the final links in the motorway chain have been forged.

From the truck enthusiast's point of view this is far from being a bad thing. There are now few enough places left where the biggest trucks can be seen working hard on steepish gradients in difficult country. The big artic is at its magnificent best as a spectacle where there are mountains. Though admittedly puny in nature's scale of things, a 15 metres long by 4 metres high profile moving up or down a mountain pass still looks like a significant happening. In places where cars are no more than ants with glistening bodies and sun-reflective eyes, where trains are merely drab worms diving in and out of dark holes in the valley side, the truck is a monster of some substance whose air of patient omnipotence is amply underwritten by the bellowing of three hundred or so hardworking horses.

However, the observer's staple diet more often than not has to be a rapid succession of trucks hammering down a motorway, meaty enough, but all the better if variations can be introduced. In terms of total motorway mileage, France, though a late starter in the standard road construction stakes, is now pretty well supplied with autoroutes, but the sheer size of the country dictates the widespread use of the enormous mileages of all-purpose roads, the Routes Nationales. So these still carry a great deal of through traffic and a trip across France to Geneva and the Mont Blanc tunnel, whether by Route Nationale or Autoroute, can reap a very rich harvest of trucks viewed in a multitude of settings. The mix of makes will obviously have a French bias, with Berliet, Saviem and Renault much more in evidence than elsewhere in Europe. British registered trucks are unlikely to be very numerous except, perhaps, close to a channel port, but there always seems to be a fair sprinkling of GB heavies on most of the long haul routes. Near to the tunnel, Italian and

BELOW: *The modern European truck on the roads in their thousands. Volvo at the Mont Blanc tunnel*

RIGHT: *Volvo F88 in the Alps*

BELOW RIGHT: *At speed, on a French Route Nationale, a Belgian truck with a car too close*

Jugoslav vehicles form a noticeable part of the traffic flow, and enough seem to be bound for Britain to swell their numbers in the region of the ferry terminals. Dutch trucks tend to be fairly thick on the ground almost everywhere. After discounting the high proportion of French built artics, the mix of makes seems to be roughly similar to that seen in Britain. Thus Volvo, Scania, Daf and Mercedes turn up pretty regularly, Fiat, Man and Magirus Deutz somewhat less frequently, Ford appear more often than Dodge though neither are very common. If a Leyland, ERF, Foden, or Seddon Atkinson shows up, the chances are that it will be British registered, and likewise the occasional elderly Atkinson which puts in somewhat of a surprise appearance. So do Americans Mack and White, but rather more often than the big 'A'. Pegasos are not all that rare but most are registered in their homeland of Spain.

The European motorways generally are much better supplied with rest areas than are those over here. Many of the parking spots over there are pleasant places set in unspoilt country and offering no more in the way of facilities than toilets and picnic tables, a far cry from the usually overcrowded British service areas with their grisly eating eating establishments and greasy refuelling bays. Outside the holiday season some of the French autoroutes carry very little traffic, though there always seems to be a sufficient flow of trucks to keep up the keen observer's interest.

Very much busier are many stretches of the German autobahn system, particularly those which carry international as well as domestic truck traffic, like the one that runs close to the Rhine between the important Swiss town of Basel and the German industrial complex of Mannheim. Though it carries many French, Dutch and Swiss trucks, German vehicles predominate as would be expected. Most noticeable, however, is the high proportion of drawbar outfits relative to artics. A rough count undertaken recently showed that the latter were indeed in the minority, there were actually two drawbar outfits for every artic. Unlike the German truck/trailer combinations of the sixties, the modern drawbar unit has power enough to maintain reasonable speeds up the autobahn gradients and to cruise on the level without giving too much away to comparable artics. For some reason the latter definitely look more impressive in action, maybe because the undivided bulk of the semi-trailer has more visual impact than that of the individually smaller units of truck and trailer.

The intensity of the truck traffic on the Rhine valley autobahnen is proof enough of the competitive edge that carriage by road has over carriage by water, despite the fact that the river was an important carrier of goods long before motorways were thought of. Before even railways were thought of, in fact, and despite the efforts of German authority to get goods transferred from road to rail and water. Despite the efforts of authority almost everywhere to do just that, so if there is an alternative to the heavy truck it is certainly not one of its present competitors. The truck enthusiast can only hope that if ever a viable replacement arrives, it will prove to be of as much or more interest to the passive observer than the vehicle it will have replaced.

Acknowledgements

Many people helped with this book. Government departments, the road haulage industry, manufacturer promotions and public relations personnel, industry chiefs at every level, drivers and all those associated with the business. Thank you all. The illustrations came from a multitude of sources although a great number came from the author's own camera to ensure freshness and accuracy. Others who sent their best photographs, either upon request or involuntarily are as follows. They are listed in random order: Weller Studios, Luton; ERF Limited, Sandbach; CAS PR, Manchester; Imperial War Museum, London; Solway Studio, Carlisle; Lucas Kienzle Instruments Limited, Birmingham; Karrier Motors Limited, Dunstable; Carl Byoir & Associates Limited, London; Renault Trucks & Buses UK Limited, London; Ford Motor Company Limited, London; Crane Fruehauf Limited, Dereham; British Rail and Oxford Publishing Company, Bournemouth; Port of London Authority; Warner Associates Limited, London; Perkins Engines Limited, Peterborough; Nick Baldwin, Ilminster; Cummins Engine Company Limited, New Malden; Vauxhall Motors Limited, Luton; Hope Technical Developments Limited, Ascot; National Motor Museum, Beaulieu; Rolls-Royce Motors Limited, Shrewsbury; L. Gardner & Sons Limited, Eccles; Geoffrey Dupree & Partners, London; Hugh McKnight Photography, Shepperton; Dunlop Limited, Coventry; Seddon Atkinson Vehicles Limited, Oldham; Girling Limited, Birmingham; Leyland Group, Leyland; Volvo Trucks (GB) Limited, Feltham; Scania (GB) Limited, Milton Keynes; and many more, most of which were not suitably credited.

Index